Also by J. David Muyskens
FORTY DAYS TO A CLOSER WALK WITH GOD:
The Practice of Centering Prayer

"A thorough and friendly introduction to Centering Prayer."
Father Thomas Keating

More Praise for *Sacred Breath*

"*Sacred Breath*, like the breath itself, creates a fresh, life-giving rhythm to its words. Beginning with God breathing life into the nostrils of Adam then concluding with the New Adam breathing divine life on the twelve huddled in fear in a locked room, David Muyskens takes us on a powerful, transformative 40-day journey rich in human joy and sorrow. There is an abundance of time and space within these pages to rest and nourish ourselves in the word of God and the stillness of Centering Prayer."

—Timothy Koock
Board Member, Contemplative Outreach

"Having read and followed the exercises in *Forty Days to a Closer Walk with God* and benefited both individually and in a group, I am happy to see *Sacred Breath: Forty Days of Centering Prayer* as yet another guide to help me continue the daily discipline of an awareness of God's presence and action in our lives.

"Each day the author guides us in how to be led by the desire to find the reality of God in us. Each day's message is based on the Word of God and enriched with the author's own experience.

"But the reader is not just left to admire the gift of spiritual intimacy with God. This book provides a simple framework for us to enter into the daily practice of Centering Prayer and *lectio divina* which makes that gift a reality, as real and intimate as our breathing."

—Elia Kwan Ying Chan
Centering Prayer practitioner, Hong Kong

SACRED BREATH
FORTY DAYS
OF CENTERING PRAYER

J. DAVID MUYSKENS

UPPER
ROOM BOOKS®
NASHVILLE

LIBRARY OF CONGRESS CATALOGING-IN-PUBLICATION DATA
Muyskens, J. David
  Sacred breath : forty days of centering prayer / J. David Muyskens.
      p. cm.
  Includes bibliographical references (p.   ).
  ISBN 978-0-8358-1031-9
  1. Contemplation. 2. Prayer—Christianity. I. Title.
  BV5091.C7M895 2010
  248.3'4—dc22   2010020341

Dedicated to
my wife, Donna

In memory of
my daughter-in-law, Karen

CONTENTS

ACKNOWLEDGMENTS

MY THANKS TO THE EDITORS of Upper Room Books for all their work to make this a better book. Thanks to Robin Pippin, Denise Duke, and Jeannie Crawford-Lee for their expert help.

I am grateful to those who read the manuscript for this book and offered their comments and suggestions: Gayle Boss, Steven Chase, Elia Kwan Ying Chan, Carol Harris, Kathy Harris, Ruth Huisman, Molly Keating, Tim Koock, Tom Ward, Don and Hilda Wilson, Jana Vander Laan, and Joy Ziemke.

I thank members of the Well writing group for their opinions: Cynthia Beach, David Beach, Alyce Reimer, and Esther Yff-Prins.

I appreciate the experience of a group using the manuscript for Lenten devotions each day and gathering once a week for Centering Prayer and *lectio divina*. These people participated in the group meetings and offered many helpful suggestions. Thanks to the following people who attend the meeting at the Dominican Center, Grand Rapids: Rich Brisson, Sharon Burtrum, Ted Damstra, Carla Edelman. Roy Eickman, Jim Felch, Terrie Heibel. Elaine Hoekstra, Moon B. Kim, Mathew Kosik, Kim McKeon, Paul Miltgen, Sr. Audrey Sanchez, Kate Villaire. Charles Vannette and Esther Yff-Prins. And to the group that meets at the Church of the Servant: Bill Bostrom, Nola Galluch, Stephanie Gerdes, Ruth Lemmenes, Stephanie Sandberg, Karen Soupe, and Carole Vander Pols. Stephanie Sandberg was of special help with breath exercises.

PREFACE

Sacred Breath: Forty Days of Centering Prayer is a sequel to an earlier, analogous book: *Forty Days to a Closer Walk with God*. In that volume David Muyskens reveals a pivotal incident in his journey. He writes about his life as a busy pastor in an urban setting in the early 1980s trying to meet the needs not only of his congregation but also of the downtown community around it. Over time he noticed chest and abdominal pains and made appointments with physicians seeking relief. But before he could keep those appointments, the pain became so severe that he hurried to the emergency room of a nearby hospital. After recounting his medical history and going through many tests, he found himself on a gurney awaiting a diagnosis. When the doctor finally came, he uttered a sentence that had the force of a Word from God: "Are you trying to do it all yourself?"

Both this book and its predecessor emerged from that experience. Central to both are two practices: Centering Prayer and *lectio divina*. It would be easy enough to read this book in one sitting. If you do, you will come away with some valuable insights from various strands of the Christian tradition and David Muyskens's rich experience as a pastor in its Reformed branch. But if you stop there, you will be missing what its author wants for you. He wants you to know what he now knows: that you cannot do it all by yourself, that there is Another who wants to do it in you and with you, and that there are well-tested practices that allow you to access that Other.

If you follow David's counsel, you will be spending a significant amount of time every day listening to the Word of God in scripture, in the events of your everyday life, and in silence, which is God's first language. Most of us will find ourselves somewhere in between the brief read and the full feast of practices. The good news is that this book meets us wherever we are on the journey.

Each of the forty chapters has a title, a verse of scripture, a meditation based on its theme, an exhortation to practice Centering Prayer, and a recommendation for other prayer based on the scripture and the theme of the day. David has read widely in the tradition. He has appropriated what he has read, and he renders it accessible to others in an attractive way. For instance, in the chapter "Selfless," David quotes John of the Cross (the soul can "walk with loving awareness of God"), John Calvin ("We are not our own, but the Lord's"), Andrew Murray, the hymn "Love Divine, All Loves Excelling," and contemporary writer Bernadette Roberts ("I see this journey as the final trek to the resurrection and a recapitulation of Christ's experiences that he realized after he gave up his self on the cross"). The verse for this day is Galatians 2:20: "It is no longer I who live, but it is Christ who lives in me." I came away from this chapter with a deeper appreciation for the relation between my "self" and God in Christ, and I was introduced to the devotional side of Calvin, among other things.

Sacred Breath touches the fullness of our lives and deaths as well. Reflection on the death of David's daughter-in-law, Karen, recurs like a musical motif throughout. (The book is dedicated to her memory as well as to David's wife, Donna.) He asks all of the human questions. And I will not spoil your reading by recounting all its variations. But I cannot resist one question he asks: *Can I forgive God?* This book comes from the heart.

"Are you trying to do it all by yourself?" That story David tells from his own journey says much about him and both of his books. It tells us that he knows that those of us who ostensibly serve God can be unaware of our true motives. It tells us that we can know about grace but still live our lives in an attempt to justify ourselves. And it tells us that David Muyskens is a truly humble man and pastor. We cannot do it by ourselves, and we do not have to. *Sacred Breath* can show us another way: a way of grace, receptivity, and contemplation. Read it. Meditate on it. Allow it to lead you to a deeper walk with God.

The Reverend Thomas R. Ward Jr.
Chaplain, The University of the South (retired)

The Reverend Tom Ward has been an Episcopal priest for over thirty years, serving parishes in Mississippi and Tennessee; from 1994 through 2005, he was University Chaplain at Sewanee, the University of the South (the one university owned and operated by the Episcopal Church in this country). Tom now focuses on the contemplative dimension of the gospel, teaching centering prayer and leading retreats. He has a special interest in fostering this practice in local congregations in general and in Episcopal parishes in particular. For the past fifteen years Tom has worked closely with Thomas Keating and Contemplative Outreach, Ltd., a network that seeks to foster contemplation.

INTRODUCTION

I CAN'T MAKE IT by myself. United with Christ, I am given divine love and power. None of us can make it by ourselves. But, just as air is readily available for its life-giving support, so God's love is abundantly given to us. We can receive the gifts of God and let go of our own efforts. It's as simple as breathing—inhaling and exhaling.

Closer to you than the air you breathe, God loves you and lives in you and wants you to receive and give the joy of life. You have a great gift. You have the capacity to know, love, and trust the One who created the cosmos and gives you life. Unwrapping this gift, you receive an awareness of God. You are given the indwelling presence of Christ, Immanuel, God with us. You are invited to let go of all obstacles to that consciousness of God and to give the love you have received.

Like breath, the spiritual life includes both receptivity and letting go, inhaling and exhaling the gift of the love of God. The attitudes of the spiritual life are analogous to breathing. You inhale with an attitude of receptivity; you exhale with the attitude of letting go, and in both you express the attitude of gratitude. These attitudes correspond to three dimensions of prayer: listening, responding, and communing. Listening, you receive the gifts of God. Responding, you let go of everything standing in the way of receiving divine grace and love. Communing, you live in awareness of divine love.

God our Creator gives "breath to the people" on earth and "spirit to those who walk" this earth (Isa. 42:5). You need to breathe for physical life. And you need a similar rhythm for spiritual life. An exercise of receiving and letting go brings you into communion with our Maker. You receive the love of God and let go of the false self, entering a transforming awareness of the One who gives life, who loves you and dwells in you.

Using the method called Centering Prayer, I receive the gift of deep joy. I experience what John Calvin called the "mystical union"[1] with Christ. I feel that union especially in two ways. Daily I engage in Centering Prayer, and weekly I attend the Lord's Table. In Centering Prayer I consent to the presence of God my Maker, Savior, and ever-present Spirit. At the Eucharist I am part of the body of the risen Christ. In prayer and worship I become one with God. As John Calvin taught, our "true happiness lies in being united with God."[2] Calvin said, "There is no other life of the soul than that which is breathed into us by Christ: so that we begin to live only when we are engrafted into Him, and enjoy a common life with Him."[3]

I pray that, as you read this book, you may richly experience this oneness with God. A brief introduction to the method of Centering Prayer follows in the next section. My previous book *Forty Days to a Closer Walk with God: The Practice of Centering Prayer* or another book will provide more detail about the method. *Sacred Breath* is intended to help you continue and deepen the practice.

As I write this book I feel a great sadness. In January 2008 my much-loved daughter-in-law died. A healthy woman of forty-six, she shockingly left us after only a week of illness. A bacterial infection so traumatized her vital organs that they shut down. As five years earlier when a son-in-law died, I suffered bereavement and faced the choice of bitter anger or sorrowful acceptance. I include some of my experiences in this book because I hope you will be encouraged to continue the practice of prayer through losses that come in life.

As I have felt called to write, each thought has come to me in a way that I consider God's work, not mine. I have written out of my own experience, including sadness and uncertainty. I invite you, over the next forty days, to read this book and follow a daily discipline of prayer and scripture meditation. It may be in dark and lonely places. It may be through valleys of sorrow and deserts of dryness as well as on mountains of fresh vistas. I pray that these meditations will encourage your continuing walk with God. In Centering Prayer I experience a profound awareness of God and receive a sense of the divine surrounding me and dwelling in me. I don't come away with a more defined theology but with an attentiveness to God that shapes each moment through the day. I don't have to fly miles away to find God. God has come to me in Christ. Jesus said, "Abide in me as I abide in you" (John 15:4). I can live in that awareness of the divine in every moment.

In her book *Prayer,* Joyce Rupp says,

Breath of life,
You ride the waves of life with me

in the rhythms of my communion with you.
You enter the comings and goings
Of each day and in every prayer I breathe.
Whether I am in the stillness of quiet prayer
Or in the fullness of the day's activity,
May your peace flow through my being.[4]

CENTERING PRAYER

You practice the movements of receiving and letting go when you engage in Centering Prayer. In stillness and silence you allow God to enter your consciousness. You consent to receive the love and grace of God. You let go of every obstacle and become one with that ever-loving Spirit. Then the love received flows outward. This becomes a way of life, prayer without ceasing—Christ received and Christ expressed.

Adrian van Kaam wrote about this prayer for stillness:

Make us attentive
To your call
Beyond reflection,
Beyond images, forms and thoughts
Into the stillness
Of a wordless presence.[5]

You can enter "a still point of the spirit to which no man, no devil, no angel can penetrate: it is the preserve of God alone."[6]

In the practice of Centering Prayer you sit for at least twenty minutes once, or preferably twice, every day in simple openness of heart to the presence of God. Letting go of thoughts, you give consent to God's presence with one word that expresses that consent. You repeat the word any time the mind wanders—not constantly, like a mantra, but whenever you need to return attention to the Holy One.

This practice will, in time, have a profound effect. Imagine yourself spending twenty minutes a day studying sales ads. In time you will develop a strong craving to accumulate more things. Image yourself spending twenty minutes a day with pornography. Sex will become a consuming interest. Imagine yourself spending twenty minutes a day checking on your stock portfolio. Your financial position would become a major focus of your life. If you watch a particular TV program every day, the tone and attitude of that program will flow into the rest of your life. So imagine yourself spending twenty minutes a day in a deep awareness of Christ. The rest of the time will become a walk with God.

In Centering Prayer you realize that the indwelling Trinity is your true center. You enter Centering Prayer with the intention to allow the Spirit to make you conscious of the Divine Presence in you and in all. The Centering Prayer method can be a doorway into contemplative prayer. Contemplation goes beyond conversational talking and listening to a deeper level where words do not suffice. This prayer beyond words brings you into a deep relationship with the Holy One.

I need that respite each day, twice a day, for both spiritual and physical stamina. If I don't have that, as my feet hit the floor, I'm running. I'm out of bed ready to get everything done I want to do today. It's easy to get caught up in frenzied activity, but I'm learning to live a different way. Wired for action by culture and upbringing, I'm learning the importance of rest. If always on the go, I'm exhausted. I need some quiet time. My physical health depends upon it. My emotional health depends on slowing down. To deal with the stress of life, I need a time of calm. My spiritual life depends on it. I can't make it on my own but depend on my faithful Savior, Jesus Christ. Psalm 131:2 says, "I have calmed and quieted my soul." That calmness comes with trust in God. The psalm compares that calm to a child resting in the arms of its mother. Or, as John Calvin put it, God invites me to unburden my cares in God's "bosom."[7]

Andrew Murray put it this way:

> The first and chief need of our Christian life is, Fellowship with God.
>
> . . . As I need every moment afresh the air to breathe, as the sun every moment afresh sends down its light, so it is only in direct living communication with God that my soul can be strong.
>
> The manna of one day was corrupt when the next day came. I must every day have fresh grace from heaven, and I obtain it only in direct waiting upon God . . . tarrying before God.
>
> To this end, let your first act in devotion be a setting yourself being still before God. In prayer, or worship, everything depends upon God taking the chief place. I must bow quietly . . . in humble faith and adoration, speaking thus within my heart: "God is. God is near. God is love. . . . God the Almighty One, Who worketh all in all, is even now waiting to work in me." Take time, till you know God is very near.[8]

When I pray, I enter a zone of awareness. No image appears on the screen of my mind. I lose consciousness of self and am given an awareness of One beyond my imagination, granting me the words to express praise and gratitude, confession and intercession. I enter with confidence that my prayers are heard. There I am in conversation with the One who is the source of all being, the eternal Lover, and the sustaining Spirit.

When I go into Centering Prayer I enter the same place. But now I do not form words but am in communion with the Word. I am in that zone of awareness in silence, just to appreciate being there and being receptive to the love and grace given to me and to all creation. No need to use words, no need to make sentences. It is the presence of the Holy One that I appreciate; and I am, as much as I can be, unselfishly present.

I desire to stay in that place, to live my life in that groove of awareness—without self-consciousness, being aware of the presence of the Trinity. Alert always to the work of God. Living in the present moment with attentiveness to the good, the true, and the beautiful. Receiving the love of God, I have love for other people. I work for peace with the courage to fight injustice. I receive joy while recognizing the turmoil of life.

Are we quiet enough to know God's ways? We can know something of God by active engagement in good work, but we cannot know God's heart without silence. Only in a silent gaze can we become acquainted with the Unknown and Unseen. Only in silent communion with the Holy One can we know who we are, that we belong to God, that we are united in Christ with the Trinity. Only in the capacity to love can we "know" the divine.

This book suggests two spiritual practices for each day: Centering Prayer and listening to scripture. In both practices, you breathe in the love of God and let go the obstacles to your love of God and all being: sacred breath.

Contemplative Outreach, the network that supports the practice of Centering Prayer, teaches four simple guidelines:

1. Choose a sacred word as the symbol of your intention to consent to God's presence and action within.

2. Sitting comfortably and with eyes closed, settle briefly, and then silently introduce the sacred word as the symbol of your consent to God's presence and action within.

3. When engaged with your thoughts [which includes body sensations, feelings, images, reflections], return ever so gently to the sacred word.

4. At the end of the prayer period, remain in silence with eyes closed for a couple of minutes.[9]

In Centering Prayer I turn from engaging in thoughts to communion with God. Rather than fight the thoughts that arise or chase them away, I let them evaporate by restating my intention to consent to God's presence and action within. I can renew my intention with a word, a glance, or the breath. This word, glance, or breath becomes a symbol that helps me stay open to God. This symbol says in a nutshell that I am open to the presence of God and the transforming work of the Spirit within. It says I want to receive the gifts of God's love and grace. With it I declare myself ready to receive divine forgiveness and to participate in an intimate relationship with the Trinity. It expresses my willingness to be united with Christ in his saving work of incarnation, crucifixion, and resurrection. A word may be that symbol of my intention to consent to God's presence whenever I become engaged with thoughts.

For example, I chose a name of God for my first sacred word: *Spirit*. There came a time when I felt led to change my prayer word to *Presence*. It seemed expressive of my consent to the presence of the Trinity and at the same time my being present to receive divine love and grace. That word has stuck with me. It helps me turn to God when I am off on a tangent with my thoughts. I also find the other two symbols for that turning useful.

Sometimes I don't need a word; just a glance toward God is sufficient. That is called the *sacred gaze*. I turn my inner vision to the One who is always present. I don't see the divine majesty and mystery, but I enter an awareness of the holy. The experience is like being in a pitch-black room and knowing that a friend is there with me. I turn in the direction of my friend and sense this friend's presence without seeing the person. Sometimes just a gentle glance toward God brings me back to an openness of heart.

The breath also can be a good symbol, as I suggest in this book. For me it has become a powerful symbol of the presence of God. As with the word, it doesn't become the focus of attention but an aid in turning to God. The breath reminds me of the presence of God. I simply let my breath be the symbol of receiving the love of God and letting go of thoughts. My breathing becomes a corollary to those spiritual movements. As I breathe in, I am aware of receiving God's love; and as I breathe out, I let go of self. I let go of the thoughts that serve my own ego. Thomas Merton recommended, "Let there be a place somewhere in which you can breathe naturally, quietly, and not have to take your breath in continuous short gasps. A place where your mind can be idle, and forget its concerns, descend into silence, and worship the Father in secret."

Always it's the relationship that is important. All these symbols fall away as an awareness of God grows, and I can simply open myself to the presence of the Trinity. These symbols are no more than vehicles for awakening my awareness of God. They are dispensable. As I mature in the practice of Centering Prayer, I need them less and less. At times I find I don't need a symbol at all. I am given an immediate awareness of God upon entering a time of Centering Prayer. But, even after years of practice, I can find myself easily kidnapped by a tangent of thought. When that happens, I again use one of the symbols to renew my attention to God.

God is here. I don't have to go anywhere or enter any emotional experience or frame of mind. I simply open my mind and heart to receive the revelation given to me. God's love is given for me to receive. And in that reception I let go. I release the obstacles to a close relationship with God and let the love I have received flow through me.

LISTENING TO GOD IN SCRIPTURE—THE PRACTICE OF *LECTIO DIVINA*

Along with Centering Prayer, listening to God through scripture, a time for *lectio divina*, is suggested for each of the forty days. These Latin words describe a meditative reading for *formation* rather than for *information*. The object of this reading is not getting maximum content as in reading the newspaper or a textbook. Nor is the object mastering the text. Instead, I aim to let the text master me. As I read, I pray, "Spirit of Christ, let me know what you have to say to me." I listen for a word from God, meditate on it, respond with verbal prayer, and allow time for silent receptivity and movement into daily activity. This classic way of reading scripture includes four activities:

1. *Read*, letting a word from the reading stand out and claim your attention.

2. *Reflect*, asking what the word you have received means for you.

3. *Respond* with verbal prayers of thanksgiving or petition.

4. *Rest* in communion with God.

The practice of journaling along with *lectio divina* can be beneficial. Have a notebook ready as you read scripture. Each day, as you take time for prayer, note the date. Write the book, chapter, and verse you are reading. When a word stands out, record it. Write out a few sentences of reflection, noting what you are hearing and what it means for you. You may also write verbal prayers that follow that meditation.

In this way, journaling enriches the practice of *lectio divina*. Writing down the word that draws your attention as well as the reflections and prayers solidifies what is received. And the writing allows you to look back at what was written, so that over time you gain insight into progress in the spiritual life and remember what you have learned.

Get yourself a notebook to keep with this book as you read. Use it for journaling each day. Record the date, scripture read, and the word received without much thought. That breaks the ice and more will flow.

A VESTIBULE

A "vestibule" of entry into Centering Prayer ignites the intention to consent to God's presence and action. Take a few minutes to prepare yourself for prayer with one of the methods suggested. Perhaps taking a few deep breaths will relax you and open your heart as well as your lungs. This breathing can be combined with some movement to bring body and soul into an attitude of consent. You can use this exercise:

> Standing, breathe in deeply and reach upward with arms high, silently saying, "Source of All." Then, let the air out of your lungs in submission, extend your arms out from your body to form the shape of a cross, saying, "Eternal Word." Breathe in, filling your lungs in expectancy, and cross your arms over your chest, saying, "Holy Spirit." Exhale, reach forward with arms outstretched, and say, "Praise you, God."

When I do this exercise, my imagination allows me to visualize the God in whom I live and move and have my being. I sense the embrace of a loving Father, from whom I receive the gift of life. I am affirmed by the risen Christ, who is with me. I am empowered to be all God wants me to be as the Spirit—the divine breath—dwells in me. God comes to live among us as Christ Jesus our Savior. I receive the breath of God when I consent to the indwelling presence, and I participate in God when I allow the Spirit of Christ to guide my living.

This exercise involves your whole being. You pay attention to posture, feelings in your body, and your breathing—not to center on yourself but to let yourself express devotion to God and readiness for intimate communion.

> Stand erect, visualizing the bones of your body. Begin with the bones of your feet and slowly work upward through your spine to your neck and head. Then let your upper body go limp, leaning forward in a slumped position. Now slowly straighten your spine, rolling your torso upward until you stand erect again. When you sit for prayer, keep your spine straight so that you can relax and yet be inwardly alert.

In silence, I let go of my imagination; I let go of myself, waiting with God, who is beyond human thought. I receive nothing except the love of the Holy One; I give nothing except my love.

Engaging in these practices requires some time. Following the recommendation of Contemplative Outreach, plan to spend at least twenty minutes in Centering Prayer. *Lectio divina* easily can take from ten to twenty minutes or more. With the day's reading, you will need at least forty-five minutes of quiet time each day. If you will make that commitment, you will be richly rewarded.

George Macdonald recognized that when we let the breath of God ignite us, an unselfish love with no desire for reward is set aflame:

> Lord, with thy breath blow on my being's fires,
> Until, even to the soul with self-love wan,
> I yield the primal love, that no return desires.[10]

Open
Slowly, the descent begins,
moving down,
down into the
corridors of my heart.
Tenderly, gently,
Consent unbars the door
of a hidden chamber.

Now I touch the
breath of my soul;
taste the depth of
my longing;
hear the echoing
silence within.

Now I encounter
the welcome
of the Divine,
pulsating, poignant,
irresistible.

Awed by the
language of God
at the center of my being,
I linger, embraced
in wordless benediction,
sheltered in the Sacred.

—Esther Yff-Prins

Suggestions for Group Use

AN EXISTING GROUP OR A GROUP formed expressly for this purpose may want to work through this book together. These comments are directed to the facilitator, or convener, of such a group. Plan to gather for an initial meeting to introduce the book and distribute it to members. The convener can offer a general overview of Centering Prayer and the forty-day plan. Point out the need to read each day and to take time for prayer and scripture meditation. Lead the group in prayer for one another's spiritual growth.

The book is suitable for any time of the year. Some may choose Lent because of the forty-day format. The forty days of Lent do not include Sundays, so these group instructions may serve as a guide for Sunday meditations during that season. Sundays could be the day for the group meeting. If the group begins on Ash Wednesday, hold the initial meeting described above on the previous Sunday.

Select a meeting place conducive to quiet meditation. Arranging the chairs in a circle facilitates prayer best. Lighting a candle in the middle of the circle signifies the presence of Christ at each gathering.

WEEK ONE

- Check in with introductions even if group members know one another. Let each person speak his or her name and state a reason for deciding to be part of the group.

- After introductions, devote twenty minutes to Centering Prayer. Introduce the practice by reading the guidelines of Centering Prayer found on pages 17–18 and leading the group in a verbal prayer. The time of silence can begin after the prayer. Use a small gong or bell to signal the beginning of silence. The bell can be rung again at the end of the twenty minutes to mark the end of the silent time. Keep time for the period of silence and conclude it with a slow recitation of the Lord's Prayer or a spontaneous verbal prayer.

- Since the first day's readings primarily concern receptivity, a scripture passage with that theme can be used for a group *lectio divina*. One choice is John 1:10-13, which points to the receptivity required to accept Jesus and the new birth that he offers. Begin the group *lectio* with a prayer asking that members of the group will hear what God has to say to them through the scripture reading. Before the first reading, invite group members to listen for one word that stands out for them in the text. A short silence follows the reading. Then invite anyone who wishes to speak out loud the word that stood out.

- After a period of sharing, invite participants to reflect on what God is saying through the word received and proceed with a second reading. After the reading a time of silence follows; then invite people to say a sentence or two that grows out of their meditation.

- Read the scripture a third time with the invitation to respond with verbal prayers that flow from the meditation. Beginning with silent prayer, indicate that members of the group may speak out loud any prayers that grow out of their reflection. They may be prayers of thanksgiving or petition and can include any concern that members bring and wish to have the group pray with them.

- After time for these responses, read the scripture for the fourth time, announcing that in the silence that follows participants may allow the word received to enter deeply into their consciousness. As leader, you will close that silent time with a verbal prayer or simply by saying, "Amen."

- Discussion may follow if time allows. Refreshments are optional.

WEEK TWO

- The group will have begun or will soon begin the second ten days of letting go. So the theme of this second meeting will be the detachment needed in our walk with God. Check-in can include members' impressions of the readings or any experiences from the past week they would like to share with the group.

- Introduce the twenty minutes of Centering Prayer with a review of the guidelines. Say a verbal prayer for entering the presence of God and letting go of thoughts that hinder communion with God.

- For the group *lectio divina*, select a passage about letting go. The familiar story of Martha and Mary could be used: Luke 10:38–42. Martha needed to let go of some worries and distractions. Or Jesus' teaching about losing one's life in Matthew 16:24–26 could be the reading.

- Read the scripture four times for each of the traditional aspects of *lectio divina* as described in Week One. You may read each time or four different voices can read. If you want other readers, invite people ahead of time, so they feel comfortable with the text. For the first reading, the group is invited to listen for a word that speaks, and participants are asked to speak that word out loud after some silence, if they wish. The second reading will be for further reflection. After some silence, each member will be invited to voice a sentence or two that comes out of his or her meditation. The third reading is for prayer coming out of the meditation time. After silent prayer, invite the members to speak out loud prayers of thanksgiving, petition, or intercession. After a fourth reading, maintain silence for absorbing the truth that has been heard.

- You may close with a prayer or a simple "Amen" and then guide any further discussion that may be generated in the group.

- This is a good week to open the way for group members to take a leadership role. Ask if, for the next meeting, someone would volunteer to lead the Centering Prayer portion of the meeting: offering the opening prayer, keeping time, and closing the period of silence with the Lord's Prayer or a spontaneous verbal prayer of thanksgiving.

WEEK THREE

- Devote this meeting to further definition of contemplation. During the initial check-in, ask group members how Centering Prayer deepens their awareness of God, both during the prayer period and at other times.

- Encourage group members not to judge their prayer time "good" or "bad." They should not expect to experience a certain feeling. Suggest that in their practice of Centering Prayer they receive whatever God gives in the moment. Generally the results of Centering Prayer do not manifest themselves during the prayer period but in the rest of life. The fruit of the practice will come in the way they relate to others and in their attitudes toward situations of daily living.

- After the introductory input from each member, spend twenty minutes practicing Centering Prayer, led by you or a group member who volunteered last week.

- Jesus' teachings on prayer in the Sermon on the Mount can be used for the *lectio divina*: Matthew 6:5-8. As in the first two meetings, a leader will guide the group through the four stages of *lectio*.

WEEK FOUR

- Invite group members to share what has happened for them spiritually in the past week. Ask what may be needed as far as "housecleaning." What needs to be discarded in order to make room for Christ? Is there an emptying needed? How would they answer the question *What is needed to have the Spirit of Christ dwelling in you?* The apostle Paul calls on us to have the mind of Christ who emptied himself and became a servant. Being filled with the Spirit of God can be the theme of this meeting.

- Take twenty minutes for Centering Prayer.

- After Centering Prayer, lead the group in *lectio divina*, using Philippians 2:5-8. Follow the process outlined in the first three sessions.

- Conclude the session with some conversation about what members are gaining from the group discussions.

WEEK FIVE

- Check in with the group by asking some questions, such as, *What insight, understanding, or experience has been yours in the past week? What have you realized in your walk with God? Has there been something you have received as a result of your readings and your meditation? Do you sometimes feel that union with Christ and the faith community puts you at odds with the culture? If so, in what way?*

- After each person who wishes has had a chance to speak, the group can be in silence for twenty minutes of Centering Prayer.

- Follow with a reading of Ephesians 2:19-22 and meditating on it *lectio divina* style.

- Close with the opportunity for group members to state briefly what each will take with them.

WEEK SIX

- As we follow the rhythm of breathing we live receiving and giving love. Ask group members to relate an incident of love of God or/and love of neighbor that they have experienced.

- Take the time for Centering Prayer together.

- Read Matthew 22:37-40, practicing group *lectio divina* with it.

- Initiate a discussion about the future of the group. Do members desire to continue meeting for Centering Prayer and *lectio divina*? If the group will not meet again for a while, a closure such as prayer for each member, perhaps with laying on of hands, can be offered. Thank each member for participating over the six weeks.

RECEPTIVITY

1   BREATH OF GOD

[God] breathed into [human] nostrils the breath of life.

—Genesis 2:7

I am amazed at the gift of life. What a gift! To be alive, able to sense the world, relate to others, receive and give love. I am continually grateful for this great gift of the breath of God.

What if it didn't all start with a bang, as some say, but with a gentle out-flow of the Creator's love? Maybe the Spirit, blowing with awesome energy, formed galaxies, stars, and planets (Gen. 1–2). We are told that a wind from God, the *ruach* in Hebrew, the Spirit of God, blew over the chaos, making order. And on planet Earth, human life began as the Maker created human-kind in the image of God, male and female. In chapter two of Genesis, the second telling of the creation story, we read that human life began as the breath of God was instilled into the nostrils of the first human being.

The indwelling Spirit breathes into us this wonderful gift of life. In each moment, you and I receive that great gift as we inhale the love of God.

Edwin Hatch (1835–1889), a professor of classics at Trinity College in Quebec, Canada, was recognized as an erudite, international scholar. Yet in plain, mostly one-syllable words, he wrote a hymn expressing the prayer of receiving the gift of life:[1]

> Breathe on me, Breath of God,
> fill me with life anew,
> that I may love what thou dost love,
> and do what thou wouldst do.

As the Creator's breath gives life to us, it purifies us and makes us one with God. Walking with God, we live in love and compassion. The refreshing breeze of the Spirit awakens us and sets us on the way of love.

> Breathe on me, Breath of God,
> until my heart is pure,
> until with thee I will one will,
> to do and to endure,

> Breathe on me, Breath of God,
> till I am wholly thine,
> till all this earthly part of me
> glows with thy fire divine.

> Breathe on me, Breath of God,
> so shall I never die,
> but live with thee the perfect life
> of thine eternity.

The breath of God glows in us. As Genesis 2:7 says, the breath of Yahweh gives life to humanity: "Then the LORD God formed man from the dust of the ground, and breathed into his nostrils the breath of life." The breath of God makes human life possible. That energy, that divine Spirit, enlivens human existence. We walk with God as we accept the divine love breathed into us. From God we receive life, consciousness, and awareness of our Source.

So breathe deep. Fill your lungs with fresh air. Hold that breath briefly. Then release the air you are holding, ridding yourself of the old and making space for the new. And as you breathe, rejoice in the gift of life. Let the rise and fall of your lungs be a celebration of the amazing gift of being alive!

PRAYER PRACTICE

In a time of Centering Prayer give your consent to the Breath of God. Breathe in, receiving the gift of life. Let the love of God flow through you with transforming power. Very soon other thoughts will come to mind. You will remember something you forgot; you will hear a sound; you will get a bright idea. This Centering Prayer time is not the time to think about these things. Let go of them by turning back to God, using a symbolic word or inner turning or by allowing your breath to remind you of the Divine Presence. No matter if many thoughts come. Just continue to turn to God. Moments of deep awareness will be given. Conclude your Centering Prayer time with words of thanksgiving for those moments. Give thanks for the loving breath of God that flows through you regardless of your frame of mind.

Read Genesis 2:4b-9 ready to receive the life God wants to give you. Let a word emerge that catches your attention. Meditate on that word, asking what it means for you. Reflect on the wonder of divine love being breathed into you. Offer verbal prayers that express your willingness for the Spirit of Christ to fill you and lead you. Finally, take a few moments of silence to let the received word sink in, giving shape to your thoughts and acts for the rest of the day.

2   LISTENING TO GOD

"Speak, for your servant is listening."

—1 Samuel 3:10

It boggles the mind when scientists talk about more than three dimensions to reality. We know width, depth, and height. Prayer has at least three dimensions. Some of us pray in only one or two of these. Full-orbed prayer includes all three: listening, speaking, and communing. All three movements in prayer express a loving intimacy with God.

Listening is the first dimension of prayer, because prayer begins with God's initiative. God's love comes first; we breathe in that love as we listen. It may seem that prayer begins with our calling out to God, but before we utter a word, the Spirit puts in our hearts a desire to communicate with the Source of our being. God has already been prompting us to pray.

We hear the voice of God as we appreciate the beauty of nature. We listen to the sounds of creation. We hear the rustle of leaves, the pounding surf, rain on the roof, thunder in the skies. All speak of the Creator. We catch glimpses of the Source as we ponder these signs. We learn the nature of the Source as we ponder these signs. We receive the awareness that we are one with all creation, participants in a grand scheme that gives us life and understanding.

We hear the word of God as we read scripture. We can come to a text of the Bible with the prayer, "Speak to me Lord, let me hear what you want to say to me." As a word comes to us from the reading, we can meditate on that word asking, *What does this mean for me?*

The word for prayer in Aramaic, the language Jesus spoke, means to open oneself to God. It means to listen, to be attentive. Reading scripture in the style of *lectio divina* makes it possible to hear what God is saying to you. Ask God, *What do you want to say to me?* When you approach the Bible with that request, you are not trying to comprehend all that is said in the text but paying attention to a word that resonates in you. On receiving that word, spend some time inquiring, *What does this mean for me? What am I being told? How does this apply to my life?* Then form your words of response. They may be words of thanksgiving for what you have heard or a petition for help in following what is indicated.

In a wordless silence you can let an insight take root. Allow the word you received to sink deep into your heart. You have the chance to move into a closer relationship. This moment of communion can shape how you act and what you say in the rest of the day.

We receive the wisdom of God as we listen to people of deep faith. Hearing their experience of divine guidance can help us see the way.

As we are receptive, insight comes. As we pray for discernment, the Spirit speaks to us in the still, small voice within. With this deep listening we receive guidance. Our intuition can be fine-tuned to the voice of God. Tuned by scripture and wise counsel, intuition receives divine prompting.

Nan Merrill published a circular called *Friends of Silence*. In each issue she asked the question *Is there enough silence for the Word to be heard?* A good question. Are we listening? Good listening requires attentiveness. When you really listen to someone, you are not already thinking of what you will say next but are absorbed in what is being said. As we listen to God, we need to be wholly attentive.

Words can come to us in a dream or an offhand remark. When they strike us, we should listen. Life presents significant encounters and coincidences, and what they say demands our attention. Surprises and serendipitous moments can take us to new places.

Sit with palms open, receiving the Eternal Word who lives in you and speaks to you. Let your inhaling be symbolic of your receptivity of the presence, love, and grace of Christ. Let your exhaling be symbolic of letting go everything that blocks your openness to him. As you inhale, silently offer this prayer: *I receive your love.* Hold that attitude for a moment. As you exhale, form the words, *Letting go of all that keeps me from you.*

PRAYER PRACTICE

In the quiet of Centering Prayer, receive the gift of Divine Presence. Let go of the noise that prevents you from being aware of God.

Read 1 Samuel 3:2-10. Listen to the prompting of the Spirit that comes through a word. Meditate on what you are given. Let it crystallize into some words of prayer. In silence prepare to take the word you receive with you.

3 OPENNESS

You are my God, I seek you.

—Psalm 63:1

Sometimes I shut down. I close in on myself. When I join a crowd of people, I sometimes resist entering into relationship with them, but soon I realize what I am missing and start conversation. Just being friendly requires coming out of self and welcoming the presence of others. I need to make space for relationships.

There is space for the love of God to fill me when I open up. I can love when I provide space for divine love to fill me. Instead of closing down, I open up to the presence of the One who loves me and everyone else. Empty lungs want air. A hungry and thirsty body calls for food and drink. The seeking soul opens to our Maker, Lover, and Indwelling Spirit. The deep longing within wants to be united with the Beloved.

When closed, I narrow my sights; when open, I see many possibilities. When closed, I withdraw into myself. When open, I enjoy the company of others. When closed, I block out new information. When open, I am eager to learn.

We can try to be full of happiness by ourselves, but it will not work. Our selfish desires for esteem, power, and security trick us into thinking that pursuing them is the way to go. Actually being filled with the Spirit of Christ fulfills the soul. In openness we receive and allow the transforming work of Christ. In complete openness we are free of barriers to receiving the love of God.

With openness we receive. From our divine Lover we receive the gift of love. "We love because he first loved us" (1 John 4:19). The living Christ comes to the door of our hearts, knocking. Our relationship begins as we follow the Spirit's prompting and open the door. With open hearts we receive the gift of an intimate relationship with God, God's grace and love. With open hearts and mind we make space for that receptivity.

British artist Donald Jackson made this discovery for himself. Jackson created the wonderful, dramatic paintings in the Saint John's Bible, which has been facilitated by Saint John's Abbey in Minnesota. The Saint John's, Bible is being copied in calligraphy, just as it was in the Middle Ages, even using quill pens and parchment. In a televised story about the Saint John's Bible, the artist was interviewed. Jackson said he was discovering his own spirituality, realizing, to his surprise, that he was a spiritual person. What was needed for spirituality, he had found, was inner space. The awareness of the spirit was given to him; his job was to make space for it. The first step in prayer is to make space.

In his book called *Space for God*, Donald Postema writes about making that space in ourselves and our schedule to receive the love of God. Shortly after the book was published in 1983 I was at a place of knowing I needed some disciplined time of prayer. I needed to make "space for God" in a stressful schedule.

Take in some long, deep breaths. Receive the gift of life. Visualize your breath. "See" the breath as your lungs fill. Pause a moment. In your imagination see the air leave your body. Let that sensation of inhaling be a symbol of receptivity of the divine life. Know that the Spirit of God dwells in you. Paul expressed this truth to the Romans, quoting Deuteronomy: You find the divine word not in heaven or a distant place but "in your mouth and in your heart" (Rom. 10:8; Deut. 30:14). Imagine the Spirit filling you, flooding you with love, instilling in you love and peace.

PRAYER PRACTICE

Silently make space for that love in Centering Prayer. With even deeper and longer breaths, imagine the space within expanding, being filled with the presence of God.

Psalm 63 speaks of openheartedness. It expresses yearning for God from a dry and empty place. David says to God, "I seek you, my soul thirsts for you; my flesh faints for you." As David receives the steadfast love of God, he rejoices, blesses God, lifts his hands, and gives voice to his praise. He meditates and sings for joy. David's experience of God in the wilderness evokes wonder and joyful song.

Read Psalm 63:1-8. Listen for a word that gains your attention. Be open to the presence of Christ; listen for his word. Respond with verbal prayer and then remain in silence long enough for the Word to shape the space within you.

4   DIVINE LOVE

"I love you."

—Isaiah 43:4

My daughter-in-law, Karen, died at age forty-six, after only one week of illness. The cause was septic shock. Her death was a terrible blow to all her family. It seemed that modern medical science should have been able to save her. I had prayed earnestly as she lay in a hospital bed, knowing her situation was very serious. The vision I received as I prayed was a blanket covering her. I hoped that meant Karen would be given a miraculous recovery, but she died.

I continue to grieve. It makes no sense to me that my daughter-in-law should die, leaving her husband and three young children. How can God let such a thing happen?

Initially, as the reality sunk in, I asked God, "Why did you let this happen?" I got no answer. No ideas or logic of explanation came. But words did come. God said, "John David Muyskens, I love you." That was my answer, a reaffirmation of the continued love and care of God. I was to live in the love of God, gratefully receiving that love and sharing it. In everything that happens God is at work. In no circumstances am I left without the love of God.

Hearing the word of God's love was a life-giving moment for me.

I thought again about that vision of the blanket. That was God's love covering Karen. And that love will hold her forever.

"On Eagle's Wings" was sung by our son's good friend at Karen's memorial service. He had sung the same song at their wedding. He will "hold you in the palm of His hand." We need to be lifted and held. God does that through the care of people of faith. With a beautiful memorial service, faith expressed, prepared meals sent, we have been supported in our grief. Words of sympathy from members of local prayer groups and the Contemplative Outreach community lifted us. The Church of the Servant, a congregation in Grand Rapids, Michigan, surrounded us in love with hugs, words, cards, flowers, and conversation. The body of Christ holds the grieving in arms of compassion. In community, God lifts and holds us.

Sometimes we let disappointment turn us from faith. Bitterness grows in us. It seems that God has let us down and maybe can't be trusted. Sometimes we don't realize the gospel of the love given to us in Christ, because we think God couldn't love us. Perhaps we feel God could not love us because we don't measure up; we are not the people we know God wants us to be. Yet the message of Jesus is that God loves each of us unconditionally.

Sometimes sorrow causes me to pray with a heavy heart. I would like to feel light and free, with my heart soaring to heights of joy. Instead, I feel down, low, with a heart that sinks. Is this prayer? Yes. As I receive the love of God, it certainly becomes prayer. I know that God is with me in my sadness. I am united with the One who loves me and whose love encompasses all. God comes to us as a "man of sorrows, and acquainted with grief" (Isa. 53:3, KJV).

Whatever your loss may be, you feel sad. You pray with a heavy heart. By the power of divine love your sorrow can be lifted. You pray with a broken heart, and through the cracks God's love can get in. In prayer you receive the love of God.

When jubilant our hearts soar. Knowing the Source of our joy, we give thanks. But prayer does not depend on feeling good. Prayer can be as natural to our daily living as breathing. Just as we are always breathing, so we are always receiving the presence and love of God. We know the embracing love of Christ even when we pray with a heavy heart.

As you open your nostrils to receive another breath, as you expand your lungs to take in more oxygen from the air, so open your heart to receive the love God has for you. Let the love of Christ fill you, embrace you, and uphold you. Inhaling silently, be aware of the Divine Presence with the words *Lord Jesus Christ, I receive your love and grace.*

PRAYER PRACTICE

Receive the love of God as you sit silently in Centering Prayer.

Read Isaiah 43:1-4. Then read it again. On the second reading, use your name and family name in place of *Jacob* and *Israel*. Hear what God is saying to you. Ponder that word. Let it sink in deeply. Offer your response in thanksgiving and petition. Take the assurance that comes to you.

5   NOTICING

I lift up my eyes.

—Psalm 121:1

I'm looking out over a sunlit valley below my daughter's home in Virginia. In the distance I see the mountains of the Blue Ridge. The words that come to me are from Psalm 121:1-2:

> I lift up my eyes to the hills—
> from where will my help come?
> My help comes from the LORD,
> who made heaven and earth.

I receive life as a gift from the One who made all things. The One whom we know as Lord, Yahweh, closer to us than the breath we breathe, on whom every heartbeat depends.

With these mountains in view I am more aware of the beauty of creation. I am conscious of the Creator. And I am given a verse of scripture that says our Maker is not far away. The Maker of the distant mountains is also near. I can breathe in the air that God has made. I can receive the Divine Presence. I am the observer and participant in holiness. A gentle breeze ripples oak leaves, a sparrow flits from one branch to another. The scene is not static but graced always with movement. Calm envelops me as I perceive the presence of the Spirit of life in nature, in me, in all. The breath of God surrounds me, fills me, sustains me, propels me.

Some moments catch our breath. With accents of sudden inhaling and exhaling, we call them aha! experiences. Surprise and discovery: *ah* exclaiming wonder; *ha!* expressing fresh realization. Such a moment may occur as you gaze upon majestic mountains, as you witness the rolling surf of a lake or ocean, as you gave birth or witnessed the birth of a child. That moment may happen as you watch a child at play. It may be a moment of deep calm that comes over you in prayer.

In these moments we see with refined vision. We see the creative work and indwelling presence of God. We become aware of the holy. Jesus asked his disciples to be witnesses. The first duty of a witness is to observe, and the second is to tell what we have seen. As followers of Jesus, we pay attention to him, to what he is doing, to the experience of his grace.

Beauty, truth, and goodness signify God. Nature reveals the Creator. Majestic mountains, pounding surf, tranquil lakes, colorful flowers all speak of their Maker. We can see the divine in humans as well. Beauty, truth, and goodness show up in human expression. We see beauty of body, spirit, and personality. We stand amazed at the insights and the love expressed by people. Emotions well up when we recognize the devotion and sacrifice of many.

God is always at work. We can take notice when our plans have to be changed to conform to the divine. At an annual meeting of Contemplative Outreach, the scheduled speaker, Father Thomas Keating, could not be there because of a health emergency. In substitution, some new DVDs that had been prepared made wonderful programs for the conference. The president, Gail Fitzpatrick-Hopler, said we were following "the plan"—God's plan, that is. In every event our task is to pay attention and see how we can cooperate.

Surrounded by evidence of the divine, I can also look within. When I enter Centering Prayer, I feel the presence of the Trinity. I receive the gift of awareness of God. A longing for intimacy wells up in me, and I am moved with awe. Sometimes the fruit of the Spirit is evident: love, joy, and peace.

The spiritual discipline of noticing leads to a realization of the love and presence of God.

A little fish asks a big fish, "Where is the ocean?" The little fish can go a long way looking though already immersed. We can look for God far away and miss the immediacy of the Holy One. The ability to sense the holy is an amazing gift. We receive it as we exercise our vision, seeing not only material things but also the intangible and the ultimate.

Reflecting on summer silence, Nan C. Merrill wrote some words of reflection for the *Friends of Silence* newsletter of July/August 2009:

> We can breathe in myriad fragrances on summer breezes and breathe away the stress of troubled times. We can breathe in sounds of birdsong, ocean waves upon a rocky shore, children's laughter, and breath away worldly noise and thoughts that bring worry. We can breathe in deeply summer's array of color—beauty for our souls—and breathe away pollution spawned by ignorance. We can breathe in sweetness as we touch and taste the freshness of ripe fruit and vegetables and breathe away all that does not nourish.[1]

Ask yourself where you have seen God in the last twenty-four hours. In what moment did you see Christ at work? Give thanks. Inhaling, pray silently, *Thank you, Lord, for.* . . . Exhaling, add the words, *I let go of all that obscures my vision of you.*

PRAYER PRACTICE

Take twenty minutes for Centering Prayer with a deep noticing of the presence of God.

Read Psalm 121. Listen for what God is saying to you through this psalm. Meditate on how you are to lift your eyes. Pray for God's help in noticing the gifts of God. Be quiet for a moment preparing to be more observant.

6 RECEPTIVITY

"I must turn aside and look."

—Exodus 3:3

In Exodus 3, we find Moses tending his father-in-law's sheep. Years before, he had run from the country where his people were being oppressed. In the course of guiding his sheep to some food in the desert, he came to Mount Horeb, the mountain of God. Something unusual caught his attention. He saw a bush aflame but not burning up.

Moses realized the holiness of the place. It had always been sacred, God's creation, but now Moses became aware of the presence of the Holy One. He stepped nearer the bush to see more clearly. Then he heard his name called from the middle of the bush, "Moses, Moses!" The One whose ground this was knew him, knew his name. "Come no closer! Remove the sandals from your feet."

Approaching God always requires letting go. Stripped and humbled, we bring no attachments, surrendering to the Holy One. In respect and reverence Moses took off his shoes; with bare feet he stood on this holy ground. Conscious of the Holy One who created mountain, brush, and fire, Moses humbly stood in awe. Later, Moses would lead the people of Israel to experience the power of God on this mountain, in thunder and lightning and in days of glorious communion. And in the same place, later, Elijah would find God in stillness.

If you look and see, if you turn aside to receive what is given, you will receive what God wants to show you. Actually, in this present moment you are on holy ground. Your experience right now is God-given. Attentive, you are encountered by Yahweh and can hear the Creator's voice. You are called by name. You must not trample on holy ground as though it is rough gravel. Take off your shoes and feel the texture of the fertile soil on which you stand. This receptivity allows you to encounter the Lord present in your wilderness. The God who has come in the flesh is closer than your breath. Every bush is burning, revealing the presence of Christ.

A humble receptivity is required—not to achieve but to receive. We choose between these different ways of life, achieving and receiving. We choose which way to pray. In the first, I concentrate on what I want to make happen according to what I think is best. In the second, I relax and watch for what God is doing.

With achievement as my aim in life, I work for accomplishments. I do it for the sake of my ego needs: esteem, power, and security. With receptivity as the way I live, I gratefully receive the gifts God gives me. I use them to the best of my ability. It may well be that accomplishments will result, but that will be because of the grace of God. I will live to receive and participate in all that God gives me.

If I pray for achievement, I will be trying to get God to do what I want. If I pray for receptivity, I will be open to whatever God wants to do with me. I will listen and spend time in communion with the One who gives me life. I will respond in word and deed to what God calls me to do. Like Abraham, I will walk in the presence of God (Gen. 17:1).

We don't invent life; we don't create ourselves. We receive and express the life that is given to us. My grandson and granddaughter are learning to play violin. When they play, they do not compose the music but follow a score written on a page. As they play the notes, they listen to their violin. They play as close to the pitch and tempo the composer intended as they can, all the while listening intently to the sound that flows from the instrument. When proficient, they are fully attentive to the music that comes forth. When inspired, they soar with expression welling up from deep within and touch the hearts of the listeners. So in prayer we express the yearnings God has composed in us; we play the melody of God's love in our hearts. Our lives become an expression of the love of God.

Inhaling, look to Christ and silently form the words, *Lord Jesus Christ, fill me with the presence of your Spirit.*

PRAYER PRACTICE

Receive the incredible and awesome gift of awareness of God. Let your time of Centering Prayer be a turning to receive what God has to give of divine love and gracious presence.

Read Exodus 3:1-6. Receive a word that comes to you through this reading. Listen to what it says to you. Pay attention to the implications of it. Take off your shoes to symbolize letting go and realizing the immediacy of the Divine Presence. Pray for guidance. Be quiet long enough to allow the word God has given you to resonate within.

7   CALLING

"I will be with you."

—Exodus 3:12

Why be attentive to God? Because it will give you a spiritual high? because you will have a wonderful experience? to get something for yourself? No. Because you are loved. Give yourself in gratitude for that love. The love God gives to you calls for your love in response. You are "called" to overflowing gratitude for all God has given you. You have been given life and love so that you can serve. You receive God's love to extend that love to others. As you receive the compassion of God you are called to be compassionate.

This call comes to each of us in unique ways—as unique as our relationship with God. Like breathing, the call comes in receiving and letting go. When Moses turned to the burning bush, the first words he heard were his name. The calling began with realizing God's love. Then Moses was given instructions for his role in the salvation of his people.

It begins for me with the realization of God's love for me personally. I come to know myself as a child of God, a person who is gifted by God. I am created in the image of God, reflecting the likeness of Christ. Being called begins with knowing who I am. I am a human "being." My being will lead to what I am to "do." When assessment of abilities and intuitive feeling match, I am being led. As Frederick Buechner said, when my deep longing and the world's deep need come together, there I find my calling.[1]

I remember making some critical decisions during my college years: choosing a major, deciding what I would do next. Diagnostic instruments evaluating my gifts facilitated knowing myself and what I was able to do. As I weighed the pros and cons of several vocations, it seemed that the need for spiritual renewal was greatest, so I decided to go to seminary. From there I went on to the pastorate of three churches, seminary teaching, and writing. God was guiding the whole process.

I quickly associate *calling* with responding to something I should be *doing*. But the doing comes only after becoming what the Holy One wants me to be. Then I can be nudged into performing the tasks for which I am gifted. My responsibilities as a grandparent, as a participant in

Contemplative Outreach, and as a church member flow out of who I am. My tendency has been to find my identity in my roles. But they are filled only as I am a person of compassion and faith. Prayer is vital to whatever I am able to do, because it fosters who I am in relation to my Maker, my Savior, and the Holy Spirit.

This One whom Moses met in the wilderness knows all that is happening with humanity, is aware of human suffering, and wants to relieve oppression and correct injustice. This God calls people to that kind of compassion, giving them creative powers to accomplish God's will. This is the One who was with our ancestors and will be with us now, guiding the course of history.

The One who called Israel cared about their welfare. The reason God drew Moses' attention to the burning bush was to say to Moses, "I want you to lead my people out of slavery. You have been away here in Midian long enough. My people need you. I have heard their cry of suffering and want to liberate them. And you are the man to be their leader."

Going back to Egypt, persuading people, facing Pharaoh, organizing and speaking were required of Moses. He was reluctant to accept. But God assured him, "I will be with you."

We too are given comfort and strength in that presence. Whatever the task, no matter how hard, we walk with God. We move in the love of God to share that love.

God calls each of us. That calling may be to wash dishes or to lead a movement; it may be to design a building or dig a ditch; it may be to pray or to work in a lab. We each have a role to play in God's creative work.

There is in me resistance to this call. I would rather be enjoying myself than to get into the messy work of liberation. I would rather pursue one of my hobbies than to get acquainted with my neighbor. I would rather be on good terms with everyone than to let my opinions of the issues of the day be known. I would like to have the consolations of Centering Prayer, but the practice calls me instead to accept the transformation of Christ. I enjoy resting in God but that leads me to the hard work of ministry. That hard work can be intercessory prayer, meeting people, raising money, helping as I am able, taking a stand. We are each called to do what we can for justice, peace, and care of the earth. Loving God means not what I can get, but what I can give of devotion and worship.

Inhaling, pray, *Fill me with your Spirit.* Exhaling, pray, *Guide me in answering your call to service.*

PRAYER PRACTICE

Take twenty minutes of silent Centering Prayer to pause and relax, consenting to the presence of God. Let the healing work of God take place in you.

Read Exodus 3:7-12. Listen for a word that grabs you. Ponder what it tells you. Consider how you are called to service. Pray for the wisdom and courage you need. Rest assured in the promise that God is with you.

8   THE NAME OF GOD

"I AM WHO I AM."

—Exodus 3:14

The call came to Moses as he drew near to the burning bush. God grieved over the suffering of his people and wanted to free them. Return to Egypt, God told Moses. There, as Moses followed directions, God would use him to free the Israelites from slavery.

Moses objected, saying, in effect, "When I tell them that God sent me, what is the name I should use for you?" God said, "I AM WHO I AM." Tell the people "I AM has sent me to you" (Exod. 3:14).

This name of God comes from the root *hayah*, which means "to be." God is. Existing eternally, immediately present, mystery beyond our comprehension. God is all that is. God is the Source of all and "fills all in all" (Eph. 1:23). Moses was told to identify the One who sent him as AHYH. I am. The One who is, who was, and is to be. The being in whom we live and move and have our being. The One who is with us in the present moment.

This name of God is written with four Hebrew consonants: AHYH. Speaking it, we might say "Eh-yh." The verb begins with A, the first letter of the alphabet (a consonant in Hebrew). "H" is a "huh" if you pronounce it. So when you pronounce the name God gave to Moses, you make the sound of breathing. You draw in a breath, EH, and you exhale YH.

Every time you breathe you express the name of God. The first sound a newborn makes is the name of God. The obstetrician listens for it. It comes first as a cry. Everyone thrills with the first sign that the baby can breathe. The last sound a dying person makes before leaving this earth is the name of God.

I find it profoundly meaningful that every mammal on earth begins and ends life pronouncing the name of God. It does not matter what theology I hold, I automatically, many times every day, say the name of God. Even if I am unconscious, I am constantly giving expression to the name of my Creator. There is never really any doubt about whose I am. I am because I belong to I AM. My existence is a gift from the One who is the source of all.

The next verse in the scriptural account, after the name AHYH was given to Moses, contains a slightly different spelling of the name of God. God tells Moses to say to the Israelites, "'The LORD [YHWH], the God of your ancestors, the God of Abraham, the God of Isaac, and the God of Jacob, has sent me to you': this is my name forever, and this my title for all generations." The word we translate LORD is YHWH or YHYH, another spelling of the name I AM. We might pronounce it *Yahweh* (Yah-way).

This most sacred name of God, YHWH, occurs frequently, 6,800 times, in Hebrew scripture.

As in all Hebrew words of the time, the vowels were understood; only the consonants were written. Later, vowels were inserted, but the vowels for the sacred name of God were not printed because that name was not to be pronounced for fear of profaning it. The vowels of another name of God, *Adonai*, were inserted, and a reader always would say "Adonai." This substitute for YHWH ascribed honor and majesty to God, avoiding the possibility of mispronouncing the name and yet honoring God.

Silently, gently, with each breath I repeat the ancient name of God. In this basic, bodily rhythm I welcome the presence of the One who is the Source, Redeemer, and life-giving Spirit.

PRAYER PRACTICE

Prepare for a Centering Prayer time by noticing your breath. Let each inhalation be a symbol of your receiving the love of God and each exhalation be a symbol of letting go, being freed of encumbrances to love God in return. With reverence and deep joy let each breath be an expression of the holy name of God. Inhale—*YAH*, and exhale—*WAY*. Let a repetition draw you into a deep communion. Move into Centering Prayer.

Read Exodus 3:13–17. Pray that you can hear what God will speak to you, paying attention to a word that stands out in the reading. Reflect on the meaning of that word for you. Pray for God's encouragement as you apply the insight you have been given to your daily life. Rest in the thought you have received so that it sinks in deeply.

9   YHWH Is a Verb

On your wondrous works, I will meditate.

—Psalm 145:5

I'm struck by the fact that the name God gave to Moses was a verb, not a noun. A verb denotes an action or a state of being, whereas a noun names a person, place, or thing. Yet the name of God that Moses was given in the wilderness at the burning bush was the verb *I Am*, being itself. God is, was, and ever will be.

The verb *to be* names God as the Source, Savior, and Sustainer of all that is. The cosmos in which I live did not come about by accident. It originated by the creative work of a divine Source. The Creator brought all that is into existence. All the beauty, truth, and goodness of the world comes from this divine Source. As I witness the beauty and order of creation, I see the work of the Creator. In what happens, I observe I Am's existence and creative activity.

And, from the story of Moses and other revelation I learn that I Am cares about what happens. The Creator loves what has been made and especially the people who have been given the capacity to reciprocate the love received. Although humans have been bent on independence, disregarding the will of the Creator, the Lord of all has provided a way of salvation. In Christ I come to know divine love. I Am has come to live among humans in the person of Jesus Christ. This act of forgiveness and mercy has opened the possibility of reconciliation. I learn that all things exist as a result of the love of the Creator because Jesus has revealed that love to us. His life, death, resurrection, and ascension demonstrate this divine love.

This love, which existed always in the triune God, moves in the hearts of people to transform them. By the power of the Holy Spirit they seek to live lives of love and peace and justice. Sacrificing self, they give their all to worship and service, returning the love they have received.

God lives and acts creatively. So the name of this God—a verb, not a noun—indicates that God is dynamic, not static. God creates, saves, inhabits human beings. God loves. God is not an object. God is no-thing. God is the Cause, the Sustainer, the Governor of all. God is in all, and all things owe their existence to the One who is our Source.

God is not a thing but a happening, always at work. The name of God given to Moses shapes our image of God. God is not frozen but always moving. God is always at work creating and loving. God is love. That is, God always loves. In receiving and sharing that love, we know God. To know God is not to know doctrine, even though doctrines aid our understanding of the divine. To "know" God is to enter a personal relationship. It is not so much to have knowledge about God as to be united with the Holy One. Faith is not only belief; it is a loving, trusting relationship.

You are one with God even though obstacles keep you from realizing that unity. You participate in being. By grace, separation from God due to sin has been overcome. Christ is God with you, one with you and you with him. That you exist does not mean you are alone; it means you exist in the whole of existence, one with Creator and creation. God's name is I Am. And you can say the same about yourself: "I am." In existence itself you are in God and God in you. This union is given by the Creator. Too often we are unaware and even rebelling against the Creator's unity. In repentance, we can turn from selfish ways to appreciate the love of God.

Psalm 145 praises the greatness and goodness of God. It exalts the "mighty acts," the "wondrous works," the "awesome deeds" of YHWH. The Governor of the cosmos is always active, the dynamic action of providence always at work. Divine love continuously shapes and moves in all that happens. You and I participate in this grand design. In prayer we become one with God. In contemplation we become conscious of God. With an awakened awareness, we know the divine love out of which the world exists. God dwells in us and works in us as we receive the love of Christ. We become participants in divine activity as we give love in return.

PRAYER PRACTICE

Take some deep breaths, giving thanks to the Source of the life you receive. For twenty minutes commune silently with our Creator, Savior, and indwelling Spirit.

Read Psalm 145:1-7. Take a word from the reading. Listen to what that word means for you. Thank God for the insight you have been given and ask God to help you accept any invitation that grows from it. Be in silence for a moment of transition preparing to bring the word you have received into your world of daily activity.

10 INSPIRATION

Filled with all the fullness of God.

—Ephesians 3:19

As a tuba and sousaphone player in high school and college, I learned diaphragmatic breathing. I needed a lung full of air to make the horn sound with any volume. Inhaling from the diaphragm filled my lungs to blow the big instruments.

We call a tall, tapering structure pointing upward a *spire*. We are in-*spired* when infused with an uplifting influence. At one time the word *inspiration* meant to be infused with life. Inhalation (also known as inspiration) is the movement of air from the external environment through the airways and into the lungs. When the diaphragm is exerted, the rib cage expands and the abdomen extends. Air rushes in to the vacuum created, bringing oxygen in through the nose or throat and through the windpipe, where the air is filtered, warmed, and humidified before it flows to the lungs. The lungs then impart oxygen to the blood, which disperses it to the cells of the body. The cells process the chemical bonds of energy-rich molecules, converting them into energy usable for life processes.

A friend of mine carries an oxygen tank wherever he goes, because his lungs have been damaged. They are less able to extract oxygen from the air, so he has an apparatus that supplies pure oxygen. This oxygen is moved into the blood stream and brought to the cells of the body where nutrients are burned. This oxygen supplement allows my friend to live quite a normal life, with the energy required.

In the prayer of receptivity, we take in the pure love of God. This gift of God through Christ gives us spiritual life. The mercy of Christ fills us and generates energy of spirit. With prayer the soul is expanded to receive the love and grace of Christ. When we exert our spiritual muscles, our inner self opens and we are filled with the Spirit of God. Christ takes up residence within us, and we receive the love of God.

The autonomic nervous system controls the ventilation needed by the body. Because the brain stem regulates and coordinates respiratory movements, we don't have to make a conscious decision to breathe. By powerful instinct we keep inhaling and exhaling. As we surrender to

Christ, his Spirit becomes the command central of our capacity to receive the gifts of God. He inclines us to open up, receive his life-nurturing love, and continue receiving that grace automatically. By the Spirit's guidance we are able to express that love.

According to the online encyclopedia *Wikipedia* (accessed 4/8/2010), normal resting respirations are twelve to twenty breaths per minute. Each breath takes two seconds. During vigorous inhalation (at rates exceeding thirty-five breaths per minute), or in approaching respiratory failure, accessory muscles of respiration are recruited for support. As much as our bodies need this inhalation, our spirits need to breathe in the Spirit of Christ. With a pattern of prayer each day and a rhythm of awareness of God throughout daily life, we receive the transforming work of Christ. We become in-Spirited, in-spired.

Hebrew scripture uses the same word for *wind* and *spirit: ruach.* The Greek New Testament also uses the same word for *breath* and *spirit: pneuma.* This linguistic link leads us to regard breathing and spirituality as similar practices. As we receive life-giving oxygen by breathing, so we receive the life force of the Spirit with openness of heart and mind. God surrounds us and dwells in us like the air we breathe. In contemplation, we become conscious of that Presence. Love gives us life, surrounding and filling us. The fullness of God gives us energy for life and service. Be *inspired*, lifted in spirit by the Spirit.

The wind of the Spirit refreshes, in purging and restoring. The love of God can sear lungs unprepared for warmth and can purge the impurities within. Divine Wisdom can come as a dark night to my impure soul. I need this torment for my purification. John of the Cross says, "This dark night is an inflowing of God into the soul, which purges it from its ignorances and imperfections . . . which is called by contemplatives infused contemplation, or mystical theology. Herein God secretly teaches the soul and instructs it in perfection of love."[1]

The second letter to Timothy tells me that I receive the instruction I need through sacred writing. Second Timothy 3:16 says, "All scripture is inspired by God and is useful for teaching, for reproof, for correction, and for training in righteousness." The verse can also be translated "all Scripture is God-breathed and is useful" (NIV). Reading and listening, I am inspired, receiving the breath of God by the divine wisdom that comes to me through scripture.

In Middle Eastern belief, the breath of a holy person has supernatural power. In the Coptic Church, officials breathe on the candidate for ordination in the same way the risen Christ breathed on the disciples when he commissioned them. For a while the custom developed for the Patriarch of Alexandria to fill a skin bag with his holy breath; the bag then was transported to Ethiopia, where the breath was let loose on the designated head of the Ethiopian church.[2]

Put one hand on your upper chest and the other on your diaphragm. Breathe deeply so that not only the upper chest but also your diaphragm fully expands. With both hands feeling below your waist, notice the muscles that cause your lungs to expand and take in more air. With that action open yourself to receive all that God gives to you of presence, grace, and love.

PRAYER PRACTICE

Enter into Centering Prayer for at least twenty minutes.

Read Ephesians 3:16–19. Read this prayer out loud at least twice. Listen for the words that especially express what you need. Ask God for that grace. Give thanks for it and take a sentence request of God with you.

LETTING GO

11 Exhalation

"Be still [let go], and know that I am God!"

—Psalm 46:10

The human respiratory system, like that of all mammals, consists of airways, lungs, and muscles that move air into and out of the body. Air fills the lungs with inhalation, then, with exhaling, the air flows back out until air pressure in the chest and atmosphere are equal. To live, I need respiration. The respiratory system supplies oxygen to my blood and removes carbon dioxide and other waste products resulting from cellular activity and poisons that get into my blood stream. This process helps maintain the acid–base balance of the body. During exhalation, the diaphragm relaxes and moves inward and upward, causing compression of the lungs and outward flow of air. Expiring, we move air out of the lungs through the bronchial tubes. This usually is an involuntary action, but abdominal muscles can force exhalation. With extra exertion, such as blowing out a candle, expiratory muscles exert pressure to send air out of the lungs.

Deep breathing promotes health and relaxes the body. You may have learned this practice in yoga or as a sport's cooldown routine. Falling asleep can be promoted by lying on your back and inhaling slowly through your nose, filling your chest and diaphragm. You hold your breath for one or two seconds and slowly release; then repeat the process until you are completely relaxed.

Just as respiration performs a vital function for my physical health, so receiving and letting go are essential to my spiritual health. As I let go, I release all that corrodes my relationship with God. I expel the attitudes that keep me from living in the likeness of God. I let go of anger, resentment, fear, anxiety, and shame.

The grace of God expressed by Jesus frees us from guilt and shame. There is "no condemnation for those who are in Christ Jesus" (Rom. 8:1). Christ is the victor, more powerful by far than any destructive tendency.

Letting go is not easy. We grieve any loss, even of things that are harmful. We can get caught in some habits of overindulgence. When good things in moderation become addictions, we have some serious detachment to do. It might be lust or greed or another harmful habit we fall into. Sex, alcohol, drugs, work, money, food, each as the poer to take control over us. When that happens, we need to let go, disengaging the desires of the false self: desires for esteem and affection, desires for control and power, desires for security and survival. Rather than tightening our own wills, we let go entirely, to let Christ be the Master, to let the Holy Spirit be our Guide. Like emptying the lungs so fresh air can enter, we empty ourselves for God to fill us. Everything that stands in the way of our relationship with God needs to go. Every thought that leads to sin needs to be checked. As the desert fathers and mothers taught, we dismiss the thought while it is just a thought, so it will not become a harmful addiction. Letting go of thoughts in Centering Prayer is good practice.

When good things in moderation become addictions, we have some serious detachment to do. It becomes necessary for each of us to know ourselves and where our addictive tendencies lie. Sex, alcohol, drugs, work, money, food, each has the power to take control over us. When that happens we need to let go, disengaging the desires of the false self: desires for esteem and affection, desires for control and power, desires for security and survival. Like emptying the lungs so fresh air can enter, we empty ourselves for God to fill us. Everything that stands in the way of our relationship with God needs to go. Every thought that leads to sin needs to be checked. Words and deeds that are sinful must be purged.

We need the transforming work of Christ, infusing us with the oxygen of love and ridding us of the poisons of hate, lust, pride, greed, and all selfishness. In the "breathing" of Centering Prayer we absorb the love of God and let go of the preoccupations that keep us from the love of God. With color, shapes, and lines abstract painters move us into a realm of transcendence. As they let go of the material world to show us another, so we let go of attachments to receive the love of God.

"Be still" in Psalm 46 can also be translated "let go." The silencing of noise helps us to enter a close walk with God. Freeing ourselves from the clamor of selfishness and conformity to the world enables us to be people who are the likeness of God. Teresa of Ávila said we must not "hold on to anything" but become detached from all things.[1]

In *Weavings* magazine Gayle Boss writes about "Elemental Grace." She shares a transforming experience on the shore of Lake Michigan. Awed by the blues and grays and greens of the moment, she loses self and all attachments. On reflection, she writes:

> Teresa of Ávila, John of the Cross, Julian of Norwich, Simone Weil—
> Christian mystics across the centuries and social circumstances, I found,
> used different language to describe the same condition of the soul at
> peace: utterly empty. Only an empty soul has room for the fullness of
> Divine Love—which *will* be poured into it.[2]

Count to four as you slowly fill your lungs with air. Hold your breath for another count of five. Then expel all the air in your lungs, emptying them as much as possible, counting to eight. Ask God to take away all that clutters you within so that you can be filled with divine love. Breathe deeply; expel selfishness, so that Christ can enter.

PRAYER PRACTICE

Spend twenty minutes in Centering Prayer.

Read Psalm 46. What strikes you as you reread this familiar psalm? What is God saying to you through this word? Pray for the willingness to let go and let God. Bring what you have received with you as you go about other activities.

12 Letting Go

"I regard everything as loss."

—Philippians 3:8

In J. R. R. Tolkien's *The Lord of the Rings*, Gollum constantly tries to grasp the Ring of power that he lost. His obsession turns him into a grotesque figure, totally destroying him. The forces of evil headed by Sauron relentlessly search for the Ring; they want its power to serve their ends. Salvation lies with the success of the little hobbit Frodo, who is given the mission of destroying the Ring. Its power even attracts him at times. Frodo does let go in the final stirring conclusion of the story. But Gollum cannot lose his attachment and is destroyed.

We like to accumulate and control. We collect stamps or mugs or teapots or properties or money. But Christ leads us to let go and let him fill us with his Spirit. C. S. Lewis quoted Augustine as saying, "God wants to give us something but cannot, because our hands are full—there's nowhere for Him to put it."[1]

Grand Rapids, Michigan, artist and sculptor Mic Carlson will soon unveil a large twelve-foot bronze sculpture of Saint Francis in the saint's hometown of Assisi. Carlson was commissioned to do the sculpture after meeting Pope Benedict XVI at the Vatican, where he presented a small statue of Saint Francis. The large one for Assisi is a peace statue that will portray the saint with a big smile, leaping over the world with an olive branch and doves. "That's what we need today," says Carlson with a broad smile. He is building a Saint Francis Sculpture Garden for Prayer and Meditation in Grand Rapids, which will house fifteen smaller statues of the saint's life that have been displayed in 2004 at Assisi in the Basilica of Saint Francis.

How did all this happen to an artist who grew up a Lutheran in Michigan? It became clear to Carlson that all this was God's work. As an artist, he was pursuing his admiration for Italian art when he was invited to see Assisi. There he went to the first church Francis rebuilt, San Damiano, and saw paintings of Francis rebuilding a chapel after receiving a message from Christ to build his church. The picture and the story of Saint Francis inspired Carlson to learn more about the saint and sculpt scenes of the saint's life. He grows in appreciation of Francis's environmental sensitivities and devotion to the Gospel. "All this stuff is in God's plan," says Carlson. "I've found the more you let go and let things happen, the greater good happens." He told Charles Honey of *The Grand Rapids Press:* "That's what Francis has taught me. We have to be open, let things happen, because we don't know God's plan."[2]

In the parable of the sower, Jesus tells of God the sower, Christ the seed, and us the soil. For the soil to be productive, it must be receptive. A hard heart will not receive the seed, nor let go enough for it to grow. A soil full of weeds will not allow the seed to flourish. Shallow ground quickly produces, but the growth soon wilts. Surrender allows a bountiful harvest by letting go of selfishness, opening to the nurturing work of God.

The great pianist and composer Sergei Rachmaninoff (1873–1943) feared touring in America. His fears of our hectic way of life were realized, and he wrote, "You know, in this accursed country, where you're surrounded by nothing but Americans and the 'business, business,' they are forever doing, clutching you from all sides and driving you on . . . I am very busy and very tired."[3]

Centering Prayer gives you a little practice of surrender every day. When thoughts come to mind, you can let go of them by returning to a symbol that says, "My intention is to consent to your presence and action, O God." You will develop the habit of letting go in favor of consenting to divine love.

I need to let go of the god who has been my servant, to let go of a god who is familiar to me, who answers my every bidding. I mourn this loss in a dark night of feeling abandoned, but this has been a false god made of constructs of my mind. I let go of the security this god provided. I let go of the feelings of well-being engendered by such a god. I let go of my mastery, surrendering to an unknown God, the Source and Governor of the universe who does not answer to me but invites me to enter a relationship of love.

PRAYER PRACTICE

Practice letting go in Centering Prayer. Let go of your schedule and give at least twenty minutes to sitting silently with God. Let go of the thoughts that come to mind by using a symbol, a word, a glance, or a breath, reminding yourself of your intention to consent to God's presence and action. This practice will give you a deep awareness of God and help you develop the habit of detachment.

Paul wrote from prison to the Philippian church about joy in Christ. He wrote about letting go of all things in order to receive Christ. Knowing Christ and the power of his resurrection meant sharing in his death, the ultimate letting go.

Read Philippians 3:7–11. Listen for a word from God. Meditate on that word with readiness to receive what it says to you. Respond with verbal prayer to indicate your willingness to let go and let God lead you. Be quiet enough to allow that word to shape your approach to relationships and activities you encounter.

13 CONFESSION

Have mercy on me.

—Psalm 51:1

Bad breath hinders close relationships. Odor-producing bacteria can grow in the mouth causing halitosis. Bacteria may accumulate on bits of food left between teeth or in the back of the mouth, so sulfur compounds enter the breath. Bad-smelling residue can enter the lungs and we exhale it. For our breath to smell good, our mouth and lungs need to be cleansed of all foul-smelling substances.

In similar fashion, to build good relationships, we need to get rid of harmful attitudes and actions. Just as a good antibiotic frees the lungs of bacteria, so the Holy Spirit clears away obstacles to trust in God and one another.

We take the first step to rid ourselves of sinful offenses when we make sincere confession. In confession of sin we acknowledge the wrongs we have done, the harmful thoughts that have crossed our minds, the evil desires that lurk within us. In making confession, we admit these to ourselves, to God, and to others. We clear the way for reconciliation when we specifically identify the wrongs we have done and ask forgiveness.

Through the ages the church has helped us define the attitudes that prove most destructive to our relationship with God and neighbor. They have been called the seven deadly sins: lust, gluttony, greed, sloth, wrath, envy, and pride. The list provides a mirror before which we examine ourselves and identify what we need to confess.

This prayer of confession for public worship is included in *The Service for the Lord's Day* prepared by the Joint Office of Worship for the Presbyterian Church (U.S.A.) and the Cumberland Presbyterian Church:

Merciful God,
we confess that we have sinned against you
in thought, word, and deed.
We have not loved you
with our whole heart and mind and strength;
we have not loved our neighbors as ourselves.

In your mercy forgive what we have been,
help us amend what we are,
and direct what we shall be,
so that we may delight in your will
and walk in your ways,
to the glory of your holy name. Amen.[1]

After the prophet Nathan confronts David with his sins against Bath-sheba and her husband, David asks for mercy. In Psalm 51:1-2, David prays, "Have mercy on me, O God, according to your steadfast love; according to your abundant mercy blot out my transgressions. Wash me thoroughly from my iniquity, and cleanse me from my sin."

Another psalm assures us of forgiveness: "The LORD is merciful and gracious, slow to anger and abounding in steadfast love. . . . He does not deal with us according to our sins, nor repay us according to our iniquities. For as the heavens are high above the earth, so great is his steadfast love toward those who fear him; as far as the east is from the west, so far he removes our transgressions from us" (Ps. 103:8, 10-12).

John Bunyan gave us a wonderful picture of the large burden Pilgrim carried being taken from his back and rolling into the abyss as he stands at the cross. The crucifixion of Jesus freed Pilgrim and frees us from sin and shame. The new freedom allows us to enter relationships of trust that bring joy. Jesus said to his disciples, "I have loved you," and invited them to dwell in his love. This great love is our true home.

As bacteria may infect my mouth or lungs, so guilt may infect me. If I have hurt someone or have made a mistake, I am guilty. Forgiveness can free me of my guilt and shame. In love God forgives. When I can't accept that forgiveness, I feel worthless and ashamed. In shame I consider myself unworthy to be forgiven. But the gospel announces my forgiveness by the free gift of God. By grace I am freed from guilt and unconditionally loved. Divine love releases me from guilt and shame.

My offense against another person requires reconciliation. Forgiveness heals the relationship. I need to forgive myself and ask the person I have offended for forgiveness. When I have been hurt, forgiveness means to accept the hurt and extend mercy to the person who has caused the pain. Forgiveness removes my shame.

Is shame blocking you from fully receiving the love of God? Name the ways you have offended God and another person. Sense the heart of

God full of love and mercy. Take inventory of the habits and attitudes that reside within you. Let the Holy Spirit be the cleansing agent that frees you of them. In prayer release them to God. Stand before the cross of Jesus where divine love pours out for you. Receive the forgiveness that cleanses you within. Feel the joy of being set free from infection.

PRAYER PRACTICE

Breathe in the forgiving love of God, letting it cleanse you within. Let divine compassion flood your inner being as you engage in Centering Prayer.

Read Psalm 51:1–12. Let a word penetrate deep within you. Take a moment to be in that place of sensitivity. What difference does the love of Christ make for you? Offer verbal prayers of thanksgiving for God's grace. Take a moment to assume a new stance for relationships and situations of this day.

14   Letting Go of Anger

> Put away from you all bitterness and wrath and anger.
> —Ephesians 4:31

I like to be in control. I kid myself into thinking that I am when actually I am not. I can't control my health. I can try to eat right. I can take the medicine the doctor prescribes. I can use supplements. I can exercise. I go to a health club three times a week. But I don't control my own heart. It beats without my thought and can stop beating any time. I can try to be sanitary, but I am vulnerable to infection. Cancer could be beginning in my body at this very moment.

I can't control events. I can exercise leadership sometimes. I can influence what happens in my family, my church, and, at times, beyond. But events happen, often quite unexpectedly. Family members and good friends have died. Plans don't always work the way I want. When I lose control, I become angry. I get frustrated when I don't have my way. For instance, I'll become angry because attending a meeting keeps me from writing. The meeting is important, but it doesn't fit neatly with my plans.

At certain moments I feel angry with God because God has allowed bad things to happen. Since God is all-powerful and loving, I don't understand why divine intervention cannot prevent tragedy. Can I forgive God? At a seminar with Father Thomas Keating, that question hit me forcefully. I resisted thinking about it, because I am only a creature while God is the Creator. Yet, the question comes down to whether I will accept what happens and be grateful that God works in the midst of the difficulty. With that attitude, when death takes my daughter-in-law or other tragedies occur, I can accept what is, let go of my anger, forgive God.

I have been angry with my country's leaders for using violence to deal with national threats. I don't understand why we, advanced and kind as we are, feel that violence is the only way to deal with violence. On 9/11 of 2001 our country was attacked. In my opinion, declaring war made the situation worse. Another option would have been to treat the perpetrators as criminals, dealing with them with force but seeking friendship with all people. Whether my anger is justified or not, I can work for a more compassionate world; and I can respect my country's leaders for the position they hold. Letting go of my anger means being free of the bitterness that can poison me and my country.

I have been angry with myself for my failings. At a forgiveness retreat I prayed the forgiveness prayer taught by Contemplative Outreach. At one point I was to allow a person whom I needed to forgive to appear in my imagination. I was surprised when the individual who came to mind was myself! I needed to forgive myself for mistakes I have made, and—receiving the forgiveness of God—be released of the shame I had heaped on myself.

When we are angry, we can choose to act on our anger—lose our temper, lash out, be destructive. Or we may unconsciously express anger in more subtle ways, such as making snide remarks, being petulant, or withdrawing. We may deny the anger we feel, but it will not go away. Instead, it will fester, and during a stressful moment, we are likely to explode. When we submerge anger, depression is a likely result.

A better course is to recognize right away we feel anger and deal with it in a constructive manner. We can bring anger to God in prayer. We can share our feelings with a trusted friend, without accusing anyone else. Anger can become energy for constructive actions.

Letting go, we let God guide. We let go of the desire to control and let go of anger. Consider the instructions in Ephesians 4:31: "Put away from you all bitterness and wrath and anger and wrangling and slander, together with all malice." By surrendering to God's will we let God set the agenda. We can follow the lead of Christ prompted by his Spirit.

Imagine standing at the cross of Christ. Make tight fists, as if holding your anger in them. Now release your fists, letting go of the anger you captured in them. With hands open, receive the love of Christ, forgiving and blessing you. Wipe your hands in complete release. Receive divine forgiveness; forgive yourself, and extend your hands to be used by Christ to offer forgiveness to others.

PRAYER PRACTICE

In Centering Prayer, let go of your desire to control, simply letting yourself be in divine love.

Read Ephesians 4:25-32. Take a word that stands out for you. Meditate on what that word says to you. Be honest about the ways you want control. Tell God whatever is frustrating you. Surrender in love to God.

15   BANISHING FEAR

Perfect love casts out fear.

—1 John 4:18

On September 11, 2001, four of us were touring the Frederik Meijer Gardens in Grand Rapids, Michigan. As our guide showed us a sculpture representing children of all races and capacities playing catch with a ball, he mentioned that the sculptor had captured a unity that was the opposite of what had just happened in New York. The guide knew about one airplane colliding with the World Trade Center before we had heard about it. Finishing our tour, we turned on the car radio and heard that the Pentagon also had been hit. Fear gripped us as we wondered *what next*? Fear struck the hearts of all Americans that day. We still live with that fear. Evil lurks in our world. We had thought we were insulated from the dangers many people face daily, but we were not and are not.

In the Bible, whenever an angel appears, the first words spoken are, "Don't be afraid." How could one not be afraid when confronted with a supernatural figure? Naturally fear arises. But God loves us, and we don't need to be afraid. Most of the time I know that is true, but it doesn't take much to make me afraid. I experience fear of public speaking, of heights, of rejection, of illness. Recalling a scripture verse can help: "Do not fear, for I am with you, . . . for I am your God; I will strengthen you, I will help you, I will uphold you with my victorious right hand" (Isa. 41:10).

My security is in God. That does not mean there is no risk in life, that we are safe from every danger. It may even mean that we risk our lives or that we are willing to die. "Those who try to make their life secure will lose it, but those who lose their life will keep it" (Luke 17:33). Letting go of a fearful grasp for safety, we find true security in the love of God.

Inspired by Psalm 62, Nan C. Merrill wrote these words:

For You alone my soul waits in silence;
    from the Beloved comes my salvation.
Enfolding me with strength and steadfast love,
    my faith shall remain firm.

Yet, how long will fear rule my life,
    holding me in its grip like

a trembling child,
a dark and lonely grave?
Fear keeps me from living fully, from
sharing my gifts;
it takes pleasure in imprisoning
my soul.
Fear pretends to comfort, so long
has it dwelled within me;
truly, it is my enemy.

For You alone my soul waits in silence;
my hope is from the Beloved.[1]

Love dispels fear: "Perfect love casts out fear" (1 John 4:18). We are secure in the love of the Holy One. This is not the security of the world. The world tries to secure peace through violence, revenge, and retaliation, tactics that will not work. Only through love can we make peace. Only in the love of God are we safe.

There is much to fear in our world. Life is fragile, and we face real dangers. We do not know the future, but divine love casts out the fear arising from uncertainty.

God's love of the world includes you (John 3:16). God loves *you*. The life, death, resurrection, and ascension of Christ demonstrate this love. Entering human existence, including suffering and death, the One who made all things took the pain of your condition and gives you hope. Our Maker came to live as a human being, fully entering the human condition with the power to transform it. By grace you come into union with God and the whole human family.

PRAYER PRACTICE

Inhale the love of God and exhale fear. Inhaling, pray, *Fill me with your love.* Exhale and pray, *Free me from all that makes me fearful.* Spend twenty minutes in Centering Prayer, allowing the love of the Trinity to embrace you, fear to leave you. Notice how you feel at the end of the prayer period. This is your true condition.

Read 1 John 4:16–18. Hear what God says to you through these words. Let one word resonate within you. What fears hold you captive? Consider those fears from the perspective of God's love. Give thanks for the love of God, and bring that love with you as you enter other activities.

16 DISPELLING ANXIETY

"I will give you rest."

—Matthew 11:28

I awake with the day's cares on my mind. Already I feel anxious. I have to arrive early at church to rehearse with the choir; I'll be leading a Centering Prayer and *lectio divina* group; I'll be going on a paddleboat ride with my church small group, called a household. I've got a lot to do, and it's already making me tense. Then there is my anxiety over the course of our nation, anxiety over the diminishment of my pension funds (Will I be able to pay future bills?).

I wish I had an eraser to wipe off all my anxiety. Today's activities can be fun if I approach them calmly. I pray, "God, help me see the fun. God, help me trust you will be there in every activity. If I can just pay attention to you, you will lead me to find the joy of the moment."

Can prayer erase my anxiety? In prayer I realize the presence of God and know that God is present each moment of the day. In Centering Prayer, I become aware of the immanent love of God, rest in God's grace, realize God is in control, and trust the outcome to God. In that assurance the heartburn dissipates, and calmness descends. This practice does not deny the concerns and responsibilities I have. They are real. I just know that meeting them will be a matter of following and trusting, knowing that I am not facing them alone. What is erased is not the concerns but my anxiety surrounding them.

One definition of contemplation is "resting in God." In quiet awareness of God we are content to accept divine control and live in the Savior's love. There we let go of the frantic pace of everyday life to linger "by quiet waters." We set aside our uneasiness, apprehension, and worry to be in the love of Christ. Howard Thurman wrote in *Meditations of the Heart*:

> How good it is to center down!
> To sit quietly and see one's self pass by!
> The streets of our minds seethe with endless traffic;
> Our spirits resound with clashings, with noisy silences,
> While something deep within hungers and thirsts for the still moment
> and the resting lull.

With full intensity we seek, ere the quiet passes, a fresh sense of order in our living;
A direction, a strong sure purpose that will structure our confusion and bring meaning in our chaos.
We look at ourselves in this waiting moment—the kinds of people we are.
The questions persist: what are we doing with our lives?—
what are the motives that order our days?
What is the end of our doings? Where are we trying to go?
Where do we put the emphasis and where are our values focused?
For what end do we make sacrifices? Where is my treasure and what do I love most in life?
What do I hate most in life and to what am I true?
Over and over the questions beat in upon the waiting moment.
As we listen, floating up through all the jangling echoes of our turbulence, there is a sound of another kind—
A deeper note which only the stillness of the heart makes clear.
It moves directly to the core of our being. Our questions are answered,
Our spirits refreshed, and we move back into the traffic of our daily round
With the peace of the Eternal in our step.
How good it is to center down![1]

"Cast all your anxiety on him, because he cares for you" (1 Pet. 5:7). We can release our restlessness because we know God's eternal care for us. We can let Christ manage our affairs. We can put our concerns in his hands.

A friend, Sue Van Eerden, was a great inspiration to those of us who knew her. She died after a valiant fight against cancer. As she waged that battle, she prayed for rest in the words written by John Baillie:

And now, O God, give me a quiet mind as I lie down to rest. Dwell in my thoughts until sleep overtake me. Let me rejoice in the knowledge that, whether awake or asleep, I am still with Thee. Let me not be fretted by any anxiety over the lesser interests of life. Let no troubled dreams disturb me, so that I may awake refreshed and ready for the tasks of another day. And to Thy Name be all the glory. Amen.[2]

As you inhale, bring to mind the words of the risen Christ, "Peace be with you." As you exhale, let all that makes you anxious disappear as you put your trust wholly in God praying, *I place my complete trust in you.*

PRAYER PRACTICE

For the moment let go of the many concerns and responsibilities you have. Put them in the hands of the Lord. Be open to receive the presence and healing love of the Spirit during a time of Centering Prayer.

Read Matthew 11:28-30. As a word stands out, stay with that word. Ponder what it says to you. Offer verbal prayers expressing your desire to accept the invitations of the Spirit you are hearing. Take the calm you have been given with you into the activity of your daily life.

17   Letting Go of Esteem

> "Those who lose their life for my sake . . . will save it."
> —Mark 8:35

Our family goes to great lengths to have a reunion at least every two years. We have done so since 1970. After my father died in 1969, I decided to call our family together for some days to keep our ties to one another. We have gathered in Iowa, Michigan, Colorado, Pennsylvania, and California. Scattered all over the nation, we live in New York, Virginia, Michigan, Kansas, Texas, and California. We come together to share our bond of family.

I need the affirmation of my family. They love me not for my achievements or my looks or my money, but just because I am one of them. We all need the affection of others: family, friends, people who care for us just because we are. How sad that some people are convinced that no one loves them. Perhaps they have been abused by their parents or suffered insults from people close to them. For some reason, they feel rejected.

Children love to play hide-and-seek. Each takes a turn being the searcher. While the searcher counts, the others have a limited amount of time to hide. The object is to hide so well that the searcher has a very hard time finding you. But most of us who have played the game harbor a fear that we may not be found. Everybody wants to be worth finding. God does not give up the search. Christ, the divine Searcher, does not fail. Our divine Lover never fails to love us.

Sometimes I try to hide, and I'm afraid to be found. I can be so wrapped in fear, anger, and anxiety that I shut myself off. But actually the Creator has put in me a strong desire to be found. I fear and at the same time deeply crave a loving, intimate relationship. G. K. Chesterton said that a man who knocks on the door of a prostitute is seeking God. Paul told the Corinthians (1 Cor. 6:17) not to be united with a prostitute but to be united with Christ. The Creator built into us a longing for God and for intimate connection, but desire for intimacy can be wrongly focused as lust, greed, or pride. Alternatively, that desire can awaken attitudes of receptivity, humility, and gratitude. Becoming aware of the Divine Presence, love, and grace in Centering Prayer, we long for an intimate relationship with the One who has first loved us.

We all need to know we have worth. But we are not saved from inferiority by exaggerated esteem. The blanket of divine love enfolds us with all the support we need. It does not exalt us above anyone else. We are neither inferior nor superior. An overattachment to esteem and affection can take control of us. Self-centeredness will destroy us.

There is another way. It is to lose ourselves. That is the invitation of Christ. Jesus said, "If any want to become my followers, let them deny themselves and take up their cross and follow me."

For a long time I wondered how I could lose myself and yet have any self-esteem. The concepts of the *false self* and the *true self* as taught by Thomas Merton and Thomas Keating have helped. My false self needs to be discarded. The false self desires control, security, affection. I am created to be my true self—like God—unselfish, loving, and forgiving, in the image of Christ. "Self-esteem" then stems from divine love, not my selfish desires. I live humbly, receiving the gifts of God. I am loved and one with all that is because of the Maker's love. I don't need to grab hold of affection; by grace, it is already given. I can let go of the false self with its exaggerated desires for esteem and affection. Even the container called self will fall away, so that I am full of pure *I AM*, a flowing stream of divine love.

In his *Golden Booklet of the True Christian Life* John Calvin discusses self-denial, saying, "We are not our own, but the Lord's." We are to "take leave of ourselves and to apply all our powers to the service of the Lord." We "surrender completely to the leadership of the Holy Spirit. . . . We no longer live for ourselves, but that Christ lives and reigns within us."[1]

Let go of your desire for esteem. Be confident of divine love. As you breathe in, let God love you. As you exhale, release your attachment to accolades and praise, and simply be an instrument of divine peace. You can use these words as you inhale: *Fill me with your Spirit*; and, as you exhale: *Free me from self-centeredness.*

PRAYER PRACTICE

In Centering Prayer, let God love you. Let go of desire for approval or acclaim.

Read Mark 8:34–36. Take a word that speaks to you. What does it imply for you? Ask divine help in letting go of the false self, becoming the true self—Christ in you. In silence, allow the word to shape you.

18 DETACHMENT

Be transformed.

—Romans 12:2

I have learned a lot from the people who, beginning in the third century, decided to abandon the world and seek solace in the desert. Especially when Christianity became popular, they resisted the pull of society to accept its values. Many went into a life of solitude to detach themselves from the selfish trends of the world. They left the materialistic society of the Roman Empire and went to live in the deserts of Arabia, Egypt, Palestine, and Syria. In their meditation and prayer they realized that thoughts led to sinful actions and attitudes. So if I can dismiss the thoughts, I short-circuit the harm to which they can lead. Like those early Christians, I can let go of thoughts to simply be present to God.

Evagrios, called "The Solitary," was born in 346 in Pontus (now in Turkey). For years in the Egyptian desert he spent time praying and learning about prayer from other desert people. He wrote 153 texts on prayer to correspond to the number of fish Peter caught after seeing the risen Christ. He said the powers of evil do not want us to pray and attempt to distract us with memories and ideas. Thoughts can lead to anger, discouragement, greed, selfish passions. Letting go of thoughts avoids those pitfalls.

I learn from Evagrios that in longing for God, I can turn away from the thoughts that lead me astray. I am freed of all possessiveness. The Holy Spirit aids me in entering a wordless and imageless communion with God. Emptied of images and concepts I can be filled with the light and presence of the One who is without form and beyond human conception. In such freedom I enter communion with the One who is greater than any image or idea.[1]

I like the teachings of another desert monk, Simeon, of the eleventh century, known as "The New Theologian," who wrote about seeing God. He talked about attentiveness, watching for evil thoughts, and dispelling them in prayer. He discussed three methods of attentiveness.

The first method uses the imagination. Standing with hands upraised one looks up to heaven with angels and saints, imagining all the images of scripture. The imagination can be a helpful method in growing love of God.

But there are grave dangers in staying with mental images. Simeon warns of the danger of pride in the skill of this practice. He also warns that one can see visions and have other sensory experiences that are actually tricks of the devil. While Simeon found the mind useful, he saw that we soon reach the limit of what human thinking and imagination can conceive.

The second method engages the mind in the battle against misleading thoughts. With careful examination of thoughts Simeon said we attempt to discard thoughts that are worldly. Mentally one formulates words for prayer. But this may be only in the head, failing to realize what is in the heart. One becomes the victim of the devil's head tricks, fooled into thinking one worthy to guide others, while actually engaged in exalting self.

The third method engages the core of one's being. The mind moves to the inner self, which scripture calls "the heart." Shedding worldly attachments, in obedience to God, one no longer lives for self but disregards all cares. The devil has no chance of enticing with interesting thoughts; they too are disregarded. The mind enters the heart and guards it. One prays from the depths of a pure heart. There one experiences the love of Christ. This guarding of the heart, Simeon says, has gone by other names: "silence of the heart," "attention" "sobriety," "opposition to thoughts," "examining thoughts," and "guarding the mind." Simeon quoted Ecclesiastes 11:9: "Follow the inclination of your heart." From your heart, with the guard of the mind, comes freedom from all cares and attachments. Simeon recommends repetition of the Jesus prayer to dispel images and thoughts: "Lord Jesus Christ, have mercy upon me." The result is a "sweetness and warmth in prayer."[2]

In Centering Prayer I experience this deep communion. It becomes easier to let go of thinking with desire for a closer unity with Christ.

PRAYER PRACTICE

Let your mind descend to your heart, praying from the core of your being. Offer praise and thanksgiving to the Source of life. Give your whole attention to Christ, receiving his love and grace. Let go of cares and attachments; consent to the Spirit's presence in Centering Prayer.

Read Romans 12:1-2. Listen for the word you need to hear. Ponder that word's meaning for you. Pray for guidance in accepting its invitation. In silence let that word give shape to your day.

19   EMPTIED

Christ Jesus . . . emptied himself.

—Philippians 2:5-7

On Monday mornings I put out the garbage. I don't like getting up early and doing that duty, but it makes my wife happy to get rid of scraps and debris resulting from a week's living. I also get rid of old papers, including notes of a confidential nature, to be shredded and recycled. The more attached I am to something, the harder it is to discard it. Glad to let go of trash, I find it harder to let go of familiar attitudes and habits. I mourn the loss of my false self. While it is false, much of the time this "self" fools me into thinking it will lead me to happiness. I find it hard to let go of the desires for esteem, power, and security that are part of the false self. When I let the mind of Christ be in me, I let go of that ego. As Jesus "emptied himself," so I am to be emptied of self. I surrender my will completely to God.

In Paul's letter to the Philippians, he repeats a familiar hymn. Paul says those of us who follow Christ are to be like him, who, as the hymn describes, "emptied himself" (Phil. 2:7). Jesus gave himself away to serve. Like him, we let go of self to be a vessel of divine love. We let the love of God flow through us. We become so empty that the self is no longer the center of our being but Christ. Paul continues, after quoting that hymn about the mind of Christ, to describe himself as "being poured out" (Phil. 2:17). Paul emptied himself so that the love of Christ could flow through him. Emptied of self, we can be filled and overflow with self-giving love. We pray that we "may be filled with all the fullness of God" (Eph. 3:19). We surrender to the One at the center who creates and fills all with the will to abundant being.

We resist letting go. The forces of evil constantly keep us attached to harmful desires. In our own power, we are unable to stand up to them. But Christ defeats them. In the strength of the Spirit of Christ, we can renounce destructive attachments and submit to the Holy One. Truly repenting, turning from sin to God, we give our consent to the indwelling Trinity. Dumping the garbage of selfishness and throwing out the old destructive patterns, we receive the love and joy of the Presence of God.

Discussing Centering Prayer, Cynthia Bourgeault, Episcopal priest, author, and retreat leader, says you enter the kingdom of God when you "freely release whatever you are holding onto—including, if it comes to this, life itself. The method of full, voluntary self-donation reconnects you instantly to the wellspring; in fact, it is the wellspring." She says that Centering Prayer "exercises the kenotic path: love made full in the act of giving itself away."[1]

In *Open Mind, Open Heart,* Thomas Keating describes how our consent opens the way for this emptying to happen. He calls the method of Centering Prayer a way of opening to God, which allows the work of transformation to take place in us. Father Keating says, "As this prayer becomes habitual, a mysterious undifferentiated and peaceful presence seems to be established inside of you."[2]

Steven Chase, professor of Christian spirituality at Western Theological Seminary in Holland, Michigan, adds that Christian tradition

> states the concept of consent in another way, that of detachment, letting go of control. We lose our life in order to gain it. . . . The very practice of prayer is in itself recognition of God's initiative and our consent. Transformation in fact may be thought of as opening and enlarging our capacity to consent to God.[3]

When we are emptied of self and our own efforts, we consent to be filled with the Spirit of Christ. Emptied of self, we become servants of God. Emptied of ego, we consent to God's will.

Let your lungs be filled completely. Put your hands over your diaphragm and feel it expand as your inhale. Then engage the diaphragm to expel the air in your lungs until they are as emptied as you can make them. Sense the analogy to emptying yourself, letting go of all selfish desire.

PRAYER PRACTICE

In your time of Centering Prayer, empty yourself and then receive God's love. Inhale grace and exhale surrender. Realize the love of Christ.

Read Philippians 2:5-11. Notice the word that speaks to you and meditate on it. How does this time with the scripture affect you? Offer verbal prayers that express your desire to dwell in the love of God. Take a moment of silence to absorb the impact of this truth.

20 SELFLESS

> It is no longer I who live, but it is Christ who lives in me.
> —Galatians 2:20

As the apostle Paul grew in faith, he no longer lived for himself but for Christ. In place of his own accomplishments what mattered was what Christ did for his salvation and what Christ did in him. Paul let go of himself, allowing Christ to fill his inner being. His identification changed from Paul to Christ. He said, "I live by faith in the Son of God, who loved me and gave himself for me" (Gal. 2:20).

We spend the first part of our lives building an ego. When we say "I," we describe a consciousness of self we want others to perceive. We need a healthy ego for normal life, but the ego is a scaffold that must come down eventually. The ego is not the building—who we really are; it is the false self. The real self is the image and likeness of God. It is not easy to let go of the false self we have constructed through years of experience. We mourn as we die to self. We suffer when we don't have our own way. This change means being empty to be filled with the Spirit of Christ.

My self is the last thing I want to give up. If I have a low image of myself, I may not think it a big deal. But my regard for myself is strong. Despite an inferiority complex, I have asserted myself over the years. But even my self is not something to which I cling if I truly give myself to Christ. Self is like the air I breathe, vital for life yet not something I possess. I will always have all I need, but I cannot possess it. Only when I exhale can I create room to inhale again. I will always have my identity in Christ, but only as I also give it away.

Paul spoke of his being crucified with Christ so the risen Christ lived in him. What self he had was not held, hoarded, or possessed but given away (Gal. 2:20).

When he fasted in the desert, Jesus resisted temptations of prestige, acclaim, and power. Followers of Jesus have followed the discipline of fasting, denying themselves food as a way to empty themselves for the purpose of receiving the love of God.

John of the Cross describes the gift of self to God in stanza 3 of *Living Flame of Love*: the soul receives God as it is emptied of self; in deep caverns the soul suffers the emptiness of hunger and thirst for God. The soul "melts away" to "live in hope of God." The Holy Spirit guides in this search for God. If a soul is seeking God, its Beloved is seeking it much more. By grace the soul can "walk with loving awareness of God."[1]

> Like the air, which receives greater illumination and heat from the sun when it is pure, cleansed, and at rest . . . the soul must be attached to nothing. . . . The spirit needs to be so free and so completely annihilated that any thought or meditation that the soul in this state might desire, or any pleasure to which it may conceive an attachment, should impede and disturb it and would introduce noise into the deep silence which it is meet that the soul should observe. . . . It must forget even that loving awareness of which I have spoken, so that it may remain free for that which is then desired of it.[2]

Andrew Murray wrote, "When you have given God His place of honour, glory, and power, take your place of deepest lowliness, and seek to be filled with the Spirit of humility. As a creature it is your blessedness to be nothing that God may be all in you."[3]

Consider the experience of a writer in California who has written about her experiences, claiming to go beyond the teachings of John of the Cross. Bernadette Roberts wrote three books based on her journals: *The Path to No-Self, The Experience of No-Self*, and *What Is Self?* She describes the complete surrender and abandonment of self in Christ to be with God. She writes, "I see this journey as the final trek to the resurrection, and a recapitulation of Christ's experiences; that is, what he realized after he gave up his self on the cross."[4] In *The Path to No-Self*, Roberts discusses six phases of the journey. By the grace of God the first three lead a person to a union with God in which one walks with God, relying on God's continued companionship. This unitive state is given to us when we pray and submit to the divine will. The nights of sense and spirit described by John of the Cross are painful experiences along the way. In the dark night the false self dies. The true self is resurrected. Our love of God is purified. In the last three phases, God brings us with Christ to death and resurrection, letting self fall away and being centered completely with God, in God, and for God.[5]

Roberts encourages us to be aware of the movement and subtle changes by which the Spirit is moving, transforming, and informing us. In this attentiveness we realize the freedom of leaving the cocoon, becoming butterflies as the Spirit moves us to self-giving and selflessness.

Pray as you inhale, *Lord Jesus Christ*, and, exhaling, pray, *I give myself to you. Dwell in me and I in you.*

PRAYER PRACTICE

Take time for Centering Prayer. Go to your deepest wellspring, your will-to-God, your true center. Allow the Spirit to empty and to fill you.

Read Galatians 2:19-20. Take a word from this reading that strikes you. Listen for what God is saying to you through that word. Are you being called to let go more of yourself? to be more fully open to Christ dwelling in you? Offer some verbal prayers that come out of your reflection and then enter the silence of letting go all thought just to be open to the presence of Christ.

CHRIST WITHIN

21 GLORIFICATION

Christ in you, the hope of glory.

—Colossians 1:27

Where am I going on this spiritual journey? What is my destination on the spiritual path? Each major branch of Christianity has its own words for the goal of the faith journey. Roman Catholics speak of a threefold path of *purgation*, *illumination*, and *union*. According to this traditional way of mysticism, the goal is to be united with God. Eastern Orthodox theologians talk about *purification*, *illumination*, and *deification*. They say we are destined to become like God. Protestants describe the way as *justification*, *sanctification*, and *glorification*. They hope to share in the glory of God (Rom. 5:2). Scripture says that in heaven the glory of humanity will be to exalt our Maker (Rev. 21:26). We move toward the city in which the "the glory of God is its light, and its lamp is the Lamb" (Rev. 21:23).

When I first heard about this threefold Protestant path, I thought it would be great to be glorified. I have owned cars called Celebrity and Acclaim. Maybe I liked those cars because their names expressed something about what I wanted. I wanted all the glory, affection, power, and security I could get, and I have pursued them to enhance myself. I have since learned a different way. In Jesus' hard and narrow way I let go of the old self. Following Jesus, I die to self and come alive as I am united with Christ. With Christ I become a child of God, suffering with Christ that I "may also be glorified with him" (Rom. 8:17).

It will not be self-glory but rather Christ in me that is "the hope of glory" (Col. 1:27). As I participate in Christ's work, I "toil and struggle" to be "mature in Christ" (Col. 1:28-29). As I grow in faith, I am "conformed to the body of [Christ's] glory" (Phil. 3:21) and become part of the body of Christ. Christ's transforming work restores me in the image and likeness of God.

Paul says we reflect, like a mirror, the glory of the Lord as we are transformed by the Spirit from "one degree of glory to another" (2 Cor. 3:18). The glorification of Christ resulted from his emptying himself. He "humbled himself" (Phil. 2:7-8); therefore, God "highly exalted him" (Phil. 2:9). Our "glorification" also results from emptying ourselves. On the way to "glorification" we lose self and live in Christ. We are sanctified in the process of being holy, dedicated as participants in God. We glorify God not self: "Not to us, O Lord, not to us, but to your name give glory" (Ps. 115:1).

The Hebrew word translated "glory" is *kabad*, derived from *kabed*, "to be heavy." We recognize God's weight when we worship. The weight of all that is comes from the Source of Life, the Eternal Word, and the Holy Spirit. We each derive worth as a gift of life from God, not by possessing wisdom, power, or wealth. Glory comes from knowing God (Jer. 9:24), so any "weight" we have is derived from an intimate and close relationship with God.

The Greek word translated "glory" is *doxa*, meaning recognition of splendor and majesty. We praise God who is greater than all we can imagine. In Christ we see the manifestation of God's glory (Heb. 1:3), and in him we realize God's love and grace. In fact, the emptying, humility, and sufferings of the Son express the glory of God. The Cross expresses the glory of Christ. Jesus invites us to take up our cross and thereby find life. Jesus calls us to humility, meekness, and peacemaking. The way of the cross leads to resurrection, so we sing, "in the cross of Christ I glory."

It sounds good (to my false self) that in the end I will be glorified. But I am not destined for self-aggrandizement. My glory is and will be to be united with Christ in his death and resurrection. As I reflect the radiance of the love of God, I become like God; that will be my glory. In the resurrection I will bear the image of Christ (1 Cor. 15:49).

Union with God, becoming like God, and glorification are not different goals. They are different facets of the same destiny. By grace the spiritual journey leads to union with God through Christ, fulfillment of the likeness of God for which we were created, and totally giving of self for the glory of God.

> We were born to make manifest the glory of God that is within us. It's not just in some of us; it's in everyone. And as we let our own light shine, we unconsciously give other people permission to do the same.[1]

PRAYER PRACTICE

Take a few deep breaths. Inhaling, let yourself be filled with the true self, the Spirit of Christ. And exhaling, be a participant in the glory given to God as part of the body of Christ. With the emptying of your lungs, let go of the false self with its desire for glory.

Be quiet for twenty minutes of Centering Prayer. Let the glory of God capture you, and consent to the presence of the risen Christ, who is your glory.

Read Colossians 1:27-29. Let a word from the reading stand out for you. Meditate on what God is saying to you through that word. Write what you hear in your journal. Lift prayers of thanksgiving and petition that grow out of your reflection. Take a moment to let the word you have received sink in deeply and become your motivation to live to the glory of God.

22   LITTLE CHRISTS

We are the Lord's.

—Romans 14:8

In Antioch followers of Jesus were first called "Christians" (Acts 11:26). The name has stuck. At first it may have been a term of derision, but 1 Peter 4:16 claims it as an honor to suffer and glorify God as a "Christian." The name means "little Christ." A disciple of Jesus becomes another Christ, united with him, though a "little" Christ. We often speak of being "Christ-like." In other words, we wish to receive and give God's love as Jesus did. When I reflect the radiance of the love of God, I become like God, I *re*-present the Christ I follow.

This does not mean, of course, that I become the second person of the Trinity—Jesus who lived in human history and the King who will return at the consummation of all things and all time. But I am a representative of Christ. Christ lives in me, and I find my identity in Christ. I offer myself to be Christ to other people. In the Resurrection I will bear the image of Christ (1 Cor. 15:49). Colossians 3:1-4 says, "Christ is your life"; and Philippians 1:21 states, "To live is Christ." When Jesus became one of us, he brought us into solidarity with him. He so identified with us that we are one with him.

By grace I am incorporated into Christ, and in baptism I have been identified with Christ. "As many of you as were baptized into Christ have clothed yourselves with Christ" (Gal. 3:27). Paul put it this way: "Put on the Lord Jesus Christ, and make no provision for the flesh, to gratify its desires" (Rom. 13:14).

In a sermon preached in January 1586, Martin Luther exhorts us to regard ourselves as "little Christs." The great reformer did not mean to diminish in any way the belief that Jesus was the Son of God. He meant for us to realize that we also have the Spirit of God in us. As God was in Christ reconciling the world to himself, so God is in each of us drawing us into fellowship with the divine and with one another. Being temples of the Holy Spirit, we each bear the gifts of the Spirit, as Jesus did. Martin Luther said we "become as it were a Christ to the other"; we are "Christs one to another."[1]

C. S. Lewis wrote in *Mere Christianity* that becoming a Christian is to become a little Christ. "The Church exists for nothing else but to draw men into Christ, to make them little Christs."[2] Originally a series of radio talks, *Mere Christianity* is a compilation of those talks. In them Lewis said, "When Christians say the Christ-life is in them, . . . they mean that Christ is actually operating through them."[3] Further, Lewis explained:

> The more we get what we now call "ourselves" out of the way and let Him take us over, the more truly ourselves we become. There is so much of Him that millions and millions of "little Christs," all different, will still be too few to express Him fully. . . .
>
> The very first step is to try to forget about the self altogether. Your real, new self (which is Christ's and also yours, and yours just because it is His) will not come as long as you are looking for it. It will come when you are looking for Him.[4]

In the way an ordinary piece of bread, by absorbing a mixture of egg and milk, is transformed into French toast, people become immersed in and identified with Christ, then blossom as an incarnation of God. Michelangelo saw David in a slab of marble. He cut away stone to allow the beautiful image of David to emerge. The true self, the likeness of God, a "little" Christ lives in each of us. This "Christian" emerges as the false self is cut away.

A Reformation document published in 1563, *The Heidelberg Catechism*, asks what one needs for true well-being; the answer is "I belong— body and soul, in life and in death—not to myself but to my faithful Savior, Jesus Christ."[5] Possessed by Christ, I have let go of self-possession, surrendering entirely to him. I am incorporated into Christ. I am a part of his body, functioning by the power of his Spirit, performing whatever I am given by him to be and do. I am one with Christ. I continue to be a human being, participating in the humanity created by him and incarnated by him for our salvation and, at the same time, I am an integral part of the living Christ. With the power and guidance of the Spirit I live and act as Christ.

With my consent, by the grace of God, I become a little Christ, a repeat of the Incarnation. As such I have a new identity and a new purpose.

You have a new ID. The same name appears on your card, but it does not call you separate and independent. You, as a little Christ, are identified as someone who belongs to him. With your breathing, pray, *You live in me. . . . Guide me as I live in you.*

PRAYER PRACTICE

Take time for Centering Prayer. Go deep within, to the place where Christ dwells at the core of your being.

Read Romans 14:7-9. Ask what God has to say to you, and listen as a word resonates for you. How is the Spirit moving you through that word? Pray that Christ will guide and shape you so that he may express himself in you. Spend enough time in silence to realize the invitations of the Spirit given to you.

23   PRAYING THROUGH THE PAIN

> . . . strengthened in your inner being.
>
> —Ephesians 3:16

Because my son had to be at the college where he teaches, I went, as a grandparent, to the middle school cross-country team meeting for parents. On the list of runners and parents my granddaughter's name appeared. She was the only one who didn't have a mother on the list.

I came home and cried. And I prayed. God was there with sympathetic love, and that was all I needed. My grief was accepted. It was okay, and I was okay with God. I spent some time just being aware of the Holy One in Centering Prayer. Later, as I recalled the evening, thanksgiving welled up, thanks for the gift of relationship with grandchildren. Prayer did not erase my grief. Grief became a significant part of my prayer.

Sometimes I pray with great pain. In genuine prayer I express that pain, and I am reminded that God cares. A sinus headache gives me annoying pain; when I sit in Centering Prayer, the pain becomes dominant; it grabs my attention. It keeps me from the calm openness to God that I want to have in prayer. At the same time, God gives other gifts of love and calm. It may be presence in the midst of pain that God wants to give me. God cares. The Holy One enters our human existence. Christ lives among us, well acquainted with our sorrows and our pain. So in Centering Prayer I come with the intention of receiving the Divine Presence however that comes to me. I may use the word *presence*. Or I may let my breath be a symbol of my receiving Christ. The symbol I use—a word, gaze, or breath—to let go of thoughts gives consent to the presence of God in the moment. It welcomes God's presence in the pain.

Perhaps you have the notion that entering the presence of God should be bliss. Instead, you may experience severe pain—physical, mental, or emotional. It's tempting to put off prayer until you feel better. Yet God loves you in your pain. Be open to receiving what God wants to give in the midst of pain.

When persistent pain becomes a barrier to prayer, you wonder how God could let you down like this. You don't seem to be getting much love from God. You can tell God all this, because God is big enough to hear it.

Express that anger in prayer. Rail at God, as the psalmist often does.

Allow yourself to feel pain or your own resistance. Bring those feelings to God in prayer. When you let go of frustration, you can become aware of God's love and power. You are able to enter a new relationship with the One who loves you, the healing process of contemplative prayer. God cares no matter what.

John of the Cross assures us that in the darkness God works to purify the soul. What he calls the dark "night of sense" moves us away from thinking to a peaceful and loving communion of contemplation. We move from head to heart.[1] Three signs mark the onset of the dark night:

- Feeling emptiness and dissatisfaction.

- Feeling that God is far away and you are unworthy, yet being drawn to God.

- Losing the mental ability to understand and imagine.[2]

The "dark night of the spirit" goes still deeper than the "night of sense." It roots out "the affections and imperfect habits" that have remained in the spirit even when the night of the senses was doing its purifying work. The radical surgery of the night of the spirit cuts out the roots that remain even when the branches have been removed by the night of the senses. It removes the sinful tendencies of the old self, still actively at work. This is a painful process. It may seem that God is absent. Yet God continues to be at work. The light of the Divine continues to shine. It is actually so bright we are blinded.[3] When we let go and surrender, by the radical transformation of the Spirit, we center totally in God. Grace, in Christ, empties the mind and heart of everything except God.[4]

What to do if you are in a dark and dry place? Keep on keeping on. Continue your daily practice of Centering Prayer not for consolations but to wait on God. Having a spiritual director will help, not for what the director may say to you but to have someone with you in the valley. Know that God takes you to a new place of deep awareness of divine grace and love.

PRAYER PRACTICE

Pray, inhaling and exhaling, *Thank you God . . . for the gift of your unfailing presence.*

Take twenty minutes of silence with a symbol that expresses your willingness to receive God's gift of love to you in this moment.

Read Ephesians 3:16-19. Be open to what God says to you through this prayer. Be ready to receive inner strength and to be grounded by the love of God in whatever may be distressing you. Bring your deepest feelings to God in prayer. Go forth with the assurance of the unfailing care of God.

24   When Nothing Happens

Be still before the Lord.

—Psalm 37:7

This morning I approach Centering Prayer with the same ambition to accomplish something as I do other endeavors, eager to discover what happens. I set out to have a time of quiet, to be centered in God, to be at peace. But I sit here and nothing happens. No consolations are given. I am still for a while. Thoughts come to mind, and I let go of them. Twenty or thirty minutes go by. It seems for nothing.

But maybe that's what Centering Prayer is—letting go, being still. If consolations come, wonderful! But if not, that's okay too. In my experience, there are times of Centering Prayer when "nothing" happens. Moments of felt awareness come at times, but on other occasions, I'm not experiencing anything—at least not according to my expectations.

Then, as I sit in stillness I realize that I am trying to be in control, to set the agenda. What I'm doing is the opposite of Centering Prayer. Centering Prayer is letting go, forgetting my agenda, consenting to God's work. With my expectations I am exerting control. If I have no expectations, I let God be present with power and love in the moment with or without consolations.

And, of course, it is not true that nothing happens. Nothing happens according to my agenda. Actually, in Centering Prayer I have consented to yield to God's agenda. Perhaps in God's agenda I am being given some rest. Perhaps in God's agenda I am just to be. Perhaps God's agenda is to love me.

Maybe I am getting it best when nothing happens. Maybe I am on to something when there is no reward for me. Maybe the closest I can be to awareness of the holy is just to be with the mysterious attraction that the Creator put in me. And, maybe when I don't even sense that, still the transforming work of Christ goes on, unknown to me. Maybe that's just the point: no effort on my part, only divine action.

Dry and dull Centering Prayer can prompt you to be alert to what God gives you. When your expectations are not being met, consider whether you are trying to take control rather than allowing God be in control. As Thomas Green says in his book *When the Well Runs Dry*, you may be swimming to where you want to go instead of floating with the flow of the Spirit. Learn to receive whatever God gives. That may not be an exciting experience; it may entail giving up expectations in order to love God without self-enhancement.

The letting go of Centering Prayer may be compared to having anesthesia for a medical procedure. You are freed from the pain you would experience if awake. The drug allows the doctor to operate without being disturbed by your resistance. In Centering Prayer, when you are quiet, you allow the Spirit to transform you. When you let go of thoughts, the Spirit works, performing surgery to rid you of dis-ease and restoring you in the image and likeness of God.

The silence of Centering Prayer frees us for the moment to be in communion with God. In the present moment, we can appreciate the love, grace, and presence of God. We can know our own being and the being of God, just being, not making anything happen.

When "nothing" happens may be just the time when you let go and let God work. God is present with power and love in the moment, and you are in touch with the deep silence of God. You are most available to participate with God when you wait. Then, by the work of God, you are united with Christ. You do nothing but receive and cooperate. You consent, simply let go, and let God do with you whatever God wills.

PRAYER PRACTICE

Take at least twenty minutes to do nothing, simply to be open to God, entering into Centering Prayer. Just be, letting God love you.

Read Psalm 37:7-9. Let a word connect with you deeply. Take a few minutes to ponder what God is saying to you through that word. Follow that with some verbal prayers expressing your need. Be silent to letting the transforming work of Christ be done in you.

25 CONTEMPLATION

> . . . too deep for words.
>
> —Romans 8:26

A grandfather told his grandson, "It's like there are two wolves in me. One is good; the other is bad. One leads me to be kind; the other leads me to be mean. One helps me love; the other makes me hate. A war of the two wolves wages in me."

The boy asked his grandfather, "Which one wins?"

"That," the grandfather replied, "depends on which one I feed."

Taking time for Centering Prayer each day feeds the good wolf, your capacity to receive and give love. When you are quiet, you receive the love of God and allow Christ to transform you from within for love of God and neighbor.

In Centering Prayer, I go to the place within where I long for a close relationship with God. I abandon the bright lights of selfish pleasure and popularity and fortune. I enter the dark place of selflessness and letting go of control. I just open myself to be with God, the One who is light. The author of *The Cloud of Unknowing* offers this advice:

> When you first begin to undertake it, all that you find is a darkness, a sort of cloud of unknowing; you cannot tell what it is, except that you experience in your will a simple reaching out to God. This darkness and cloud . . . prevents you from seeing [God] clearly by the light of understanding in your reason, and from experiencing [God] in sweetness of love in your affection. So set yourself to rest in this darkness as long as you can, always crying out after [God] whom you love.[1]

In contemplative prayer we enter that deep longing for God. Not by reason or emotion but by simple consent to Divine Presence, we become aware of God. We have been given the capacity to be aware of God. Traditionally we call that gift "contemplation." This awareness of God may not be a "felt" presence, because Divine Presence does not depend on whether we feel it or not. With this gift of gentle awareness we receive the love of our Creator who has come to rescue us through Christ.

In *contemplative prayer*, we silently, without words, become aware of divine grace and love. In *petitionary prayer*, we often use words. In *listening prayer*, we may receive messages in words. By contrast, in *contemplation* we may use no words at all, simply enjoying communion.

Contemplation may be defined as "the fixed gaze upon the Unknown, a long and loving look at the Real." In contemplative prayer we let go of all else, just receiving the loving presence of our triune God. We simply "rest in God."

Steven Chase wrote about the Victorine spiritual tradition of the Middle Ages. The Victorines' greatest teacher, Richard, called contemplation "suspension in wonder over the many manifestations of divine wisdom." Chase comments:

> Today, in our busy, technological, scientific, narcissistic, and skeptical age, it is difficult, even counter-cultural, to cultivate mystery and wonder. Wonder requires that we admit that something is beyond the ken of our understanding, beyond our personal control. Yet today there is also renewed interest in, and even a craving for, a return of wonder and awe.[2]

Contemplative prayer leads to contemplative living. A daily practice of contemplative prayer empowers us to participate in the divine nature. It cultivates the fruit of the Spirit—love, joy and peace, kindness and generosity.

With contemplative awareness we gain the capacity to notice our own behavior, and to change it when we are following a destructive impulse. We become more sharply conscious of the will of God. We become more closely united with Christ. We see more clearly how Christ is at work. We experience more readily the love of the gospel. We perceive expressions of the love of the Trinity. With this awareness we practice contemplative living.

Thomas Kelly, Quaker missionary, educator, and scholar, testified to the peace and joy that result from contemplation

> when life is lived with singleness of eye, for a holy Center where the breath and stillness of Eternity are heavy upon us and we are wholly yielded to [God]. . . . It is the Eternal Goodness calling you to return Home. . . . It is the life *beyond* fevered strain. We are called beyond strain, to peace and power and joy and love and through abandonment of self. . . .
>
> But if we *center down*, as the old phrase goes, and live in that holy Silence that is dearer than life, and take our life program into the silent places of the heart, with complete openness, ready to do, ready to renounce according to His leading, then many of the things we are doing lose their vitality for us.[3]

PRAYER PRACTICE

Breathe deep, aware of the core of your being. Inhaling, let yourself receive the deep joy of being united with Christ. Exhaling, release the many desires of the ego.

In a time of Centering Prayer, be in wonder, receiving the love of God. Let go of all thoughts that take you away from being in awe of our Source, Savior, and Holy Spirit.

Read Romans 8:26–27. Let God speak to you through these words. Take a word that stands out in the reading and meditate on its meaning. Ask for help in applying that message to your daily living. Give a little time to being in contemplation of the wonder and majesty of the Holy One.

26 TRUSTING GOD

> Trust in [God] at all times.
>
> —Psalm 62:8

In the wake of financial distress, many have lost confidence in the U.S. economy. "In God we trust" says every U.S. coin. What does this mean? Does it mean that we expect God to be good to us? Are we expecting that God will do what we think should happen? Are we affirming that we think God wants to bless us more than others?

I find myself sometimes moving into a dark mood: I'm worried about my health; I'm pessimistic about the future; I'm feeling distressed about my ability to meet the challenges a day brings. When I find myself moving toward these thoughts, *the welcoming prayer* can change my mood. Contemplative Outreach, the community that supports Centering Prayer, teaches the welcoming prayer as a way to meet the challenges of each day. This prayer acknowledges the presence of providence in the encounters of daily life.

In the welcoming prayer, I say welcome to the presence of God in the situation. I know that Presence means love, joy, and peace can be given in the circumstance, actually are present already; and I experience that fruit of the Spirit. I can let go of the desires for esteem, power, and security that were driving me to the dark place. Instead, I accept the situation with trust.

What do I mean by trusting in God? Not that God will do what I want but rather that I accept what is, trusting that God will be with me no matter what happens. Evil in the world can certainly mess things up, but the Holy One actually controls what happens. I trust that going along with divine providence everything will be all right. With trust I am free from the need to control. In trust I let go and let things be, knowing that I am held in the embrace of divine love.

The shift has been a dramatic one for me. It came in the wake of losing two beloved members of my family—first, a son-in-law and, then, my daughter-in-law. I felt God had let us down and wondered whether I could trust God if God let such untimely, tragic things happen. I came to realize that trust in God does not mean confidence that nothing bad can happen. Trust means knowing God is there in the midst of events. Trust means welcoming the love of God, which provides strength in whatever takes place. I believe that God is present in every moment.

As I practice the welcoming prayer, I first sink into the distress I am feeling. I notice where I feel pain in my body. My body stores much wisdom. I tap that wisdom residing in me. I become aware of any discomfort—a tight shoulder, tense thighs, unease in the digestive track, a headache. I let myself be aware of the origin of the pain I feel. This process may take some time, or it can be almost instantaneous as when I am suddenly faced with a difficult circumstance.

After identifying the situation, I say, "Welcome." That becomes my prayer word in activity. I repeat, "Welcome, welcome, welcome," ready to see how God is at work in what is happening.

With this word *welcome* we surrender to God's will. As Jean-Pierre de Caussade (1675–1751) said, we abandon ourselves to divine providence. He taught:

> Obedience to God's undefined will depends entirely on our passive surrender to it. We put nothing of ourselves into it apart from a general willingness that is prepared to do anything or nothing, like a tool that, though it has no power in itself, when in the hands of the craftsman, can be used by him for any purpose within the range of its capacity and design. . . . so we leave God to act in everything, reserving for ourselves only love and obedience to the present moment.[1]

After taking a welcoming attitude, in the next step, I let go of selfish desires. My false self wants to grab affection, to take control, and to seek security. Submission to the will of God demands letting go of those desires. I consciously reinforce this letting go. Like breathing, I receive and let go: receive the grace of God and let go of all that interferes with my cooperation with divine action.

The welcoming prayer method, as taught by Contemplative Outreach, has three steps. You can copy them on a card to take with you:

Focus, feel, and sink into the feelings, emotions, thoughts, sensations, and commentaries in your body.

Welcome the Divine Indwelling in the feelings, emotions, thoughts, commentaries or sensations in your body by saying, "Welcome."

Let go by repeating the following sentences:

- "I let go of the desire for security, affection, control."
- "I let go of the desire to change this feeling/sensation."[2]

Of course, God may change the situation. But that is God's work, not mine. I accept the pain or distress, knowing that the Beloved is present and active in that moment. I'm happy when I "trust and obey," says the gospel song. To trust in God does not mean to trust God to act as I like. Rather it is to trust God to act as God likes. With trust, I surrender to God's action. I live with contentment, accepting what is given.

Practice the welcoming prayer by following the three steps above.

PRAYER PRACTICE

In Centering Prayer, use your symbol of consent to God as you need it to let go of thoughts and be with God in faith and love.

Read Psalm 62:1–8. Take the word that grabs your attention and meditate on it, seeking what is being said to you through it. Put in words the prayers that flow from that reflection. Be in silence to let trust in God grow in you.

27 THE AROMA OF CHRIST

. . . a fragrance from life to life.

—2 Corinthians 2:16

After a harsh Michigan winter I enjoy the fresh air of spring days. I get out to do some yard work and smell the aroma of fresh growth and blossoming crocus and tulips. Pleasant smells can be exhilarating. People have considered some odors pleasant and others offensive since earliest history. Archaeologists have discovered perfumes dating back more than four thousand years. Ancient peoples created pleasant fragrances with a variety of herbs and spices, from almond to conifer resin.[1]

I smell odors in the air because my nostrils contain instruments that gather the information. Tiny hairs in my nose filter the air I breathe, and air passes through a layer of mucous to the olfactory bulb. Nerve cells send signals along the olfactory nerve to the brain, where they are interpreted and I recognize smells. Some are attractive, some repellant.[2] Some foods seem more appetizing than others because they emit a pleasant aroma. I learn from science that, on an unconscious level, people are attracted or repelled to one another by smell. I remember some smells long after events and words have faded from conscious memory. For example, farm smells still can take me back to childhood visits to my Uncle Henry's farm.

Just as a fragrance—invisible, permeating, and highly evocative—can affect us deeply, what Paul calls the "aroma of Christ" has the power to spread joy. When I receive the fragrance of Christ, I am drawn to union with him, much the way fragrance draws together the lovers in the Song of Solomon. The grace I receive is profoundly life-giving.

Whether we are aware of it or not, God and others notice our unity with Christ. The prophecy of Hosea says through repentance and forgiveness Israel will become fragrant to God (Hos. 14:4-7). The second letter of Paul to the Corinthians talks about the fragrance we emit when we know God and says we become "the aroma of Christ to God among those who are being saved" (2 Cor. 2:15).

Along with other early fathers of the church, Origen wrote about the fragrance of Christ, transmitted by his followers. Origen quotes

Psalm 45:7: "God, your God, has anointed you with the oil of gladness." He says this anointing becomes the fragrance of those who partake in Christ. Christ is the vessel who contains this pleasant smelling oil. And his followers "will be partakers and receivers of His odour, in proportion to their nearness to the vessel."[3]

In his *Confessions*, Augustine describes his conversion to love for God. Restless and searching, he "returned" to God, who actually had been with him all along. In Augustine's awakening, all his senses were overwhelmed, including smell. He writes:

> Thou wert with me, but I was not with Thee. . . . Thou called, and shouted, and burst my deafness. Thou flashed, shone, and scattered my blindness. Thou breathed odors, and I drew in breath and panted for Thee. I tasted, and hunger and thirst. Thou touched me, and I burned for Thy peace.[4]

Eastern Orthodox worship calls on all five senses in awareness of God. To awaken the sense of smell, the odor of incense fills the sanctuary. The love of God, Jesus said, involves the whole self—mind and heart as well as physical strength.

When we witness to Jesus and his work, we share the fragrance of Christ with others. We convey his love and demonstrate his compassion. A prayer by John Henry Newman is recited every day by Mother Teresa's Missionaries of Charity, asking for the fragrance of Christ:

> Dear Jesus, help us to spread your fragrance
> everywhere we go.
> Flood our souls with your spirit and life.
> Penetrate and possess our whole being so utterly
> that our lives may be a radiance of yours.
> Shine through us and be so in us that every soul
> we come in contact with
> may feel your
> presence in our soul.[5]

May our prayer be to spread the aroma of Christ. May we encourage a sense of God by our faith and daily walk. Begin a daily pattern of welcoming the grace of God in each moment. Notice the fragrance of divine love. Reaffirm your willingness to be an expression of love for others.

PRAYER PRACTICE

Take the time for Centering Prayer to receive the fragrance of God's love and let that love flow out from you in love for God and others.

Read 2 Corinthians 2:14–17. Listen for what God has to say to you in this text. Give some thought to your aroma as a follower of Jesus Christ. What fragrance would you like to transmit? Pray for God's help in having a loving influence on the people with whom you connect. Let the word God has given you sink in deep to transform you.

28 Wind

"The wind blows where it chooses."

—John 3:8

I like sailing a little board boat on a lake. There is no motor to propel the boat. If the boat moves at all, the power comes from the wind. On a still day, sails catch no wind and so the boat can go nowhere. When the wind is strong, the boat moves along quickly. Since I sit right at the surface of the water, sailing in the board boat seems faster than sailing in a large boat. The harder the wind blows, the faster the boat can go. Of course, there is a point where the wind can be too much for the little boat. I have capsized several times, sending prescription sunglasses to the bottom of the lake. I have had to swim, right the boat, get back on, and sail again—this time more careful of catching too much wind.

With the wind powering my little sailboat, I can go almost anywhere on the lake. If I want to go in a direction against the wind, I tack across the wind by moving into the wind enough each time so eventually I reach my desired destination. Actually, I move fastest across the wind. Going with the wind can be fun too, with sails out, harnessing as much power as possible.

Sailing requires constant attention to the wind. If the wind swirls, I have to adjust the rudder. In a gusty wind, I have to adjust the sails. For maximum speed, I can shift my weight in the boat to hold down the windward side. With a strong wind there is never a moment I can let go of my attention.

In the Spirit-led life, the wind of God—the breath of the Spirit—propels me. Jesus explained the life of being born from above to Nicodemus: "The wind blows where it chooses, and you hear the sound of it, but you do not know where it comes from or where it goes. So it is with everyone who is born of the Spirit" (John 3:8). As the wind blows with power and mystery, so the Spirit of God moves powerfully and mysteriously. As a disciple of Christ, I allow the wind of God to shape who I am and where I go.

My favorite place to practice Centering Prayer at home is next to the fireplace. Over the mantle hangs a wooden hull that I carved, with a cross for the mast. It reminds me that the Spirit of Christ directs my life. I move with power as the Spirit moves me. My dad liked to tell stories about the power of the wind. He had seen pieces of straw imbedded in a fence post by strong winds and told about seeing one building demolished by wind while the structure next to it was not touched. Like my father, I remember a tornado coming through in Minnesota. A dark, eerie calm preceded the storm, and then the wind hit. We did not know if our house could withstand its fury. Just a half-mile away, a farm was totally obliterated. The family auto was blown out into a field several hundred feet from where it had been parked. Our family grew to have great respect for wind through that experience.

Not paying attention to the wind risks being blown away. Psalm 1 says the wicked "are like chaff that the wind drives away" (Ps. 1:4). Wind can bring clouds producing rain to water the earth. It can bring cold air and snow, or it can bring warm air and sunny days. When we pay attention to the wind, we are more likely to act appropriately. On the steeple of the church where I was pastor for twenty-four years sits a weather vane. Before radio and TV weather news, people watched for the wind direction. It could tell them much about the weather to be expected. A northwesterly wind brought cold. An easterly wind brought warmth and humidity from the ocean. I live with power, love, and joy as I attend to the way the Spirit of Christ is moving.

Some people harness the power of wind to produce electricity. I have driven through parts of the Netherlands and Germany where wind turbines fill the horizon. In parts of Iowa and Illinois, these stately turbines take the power of the wind to create electricity for energy and light.

Because the word rendered spirit in the scriptures denotes wind, air, breath, as well as Spirit, the operations of the Holy Spirit are compared to the wind (John 3:8; Acts 2:2). At Pentecost, when they heard the sound of a mighty wind, the disciples knew that the Spirit was being poured out on them. As Jesus had promised, the power of the Spirit energized them. It drove them to take the gospel to the ends of the earth.

We each need energy for normal life. When we breathe, we draw life-giving air into our bodies. So we receive the oxygen needed to fuel our cells and give us life. Similarly, the Holy Spirit empowers us. In prayer we can open ourselves to that indwelling Spirit, the wind that motivates and encourages us.

The words of the hymn "Wind Who Makes All Winds that Blow" by Thomas H. Troeger say it well:

Wind who makes all winds that blow—
gusts that bend the saplings low,
gales that heave the sea in waves,
stirrings in the mind's deep caves—
aim your breath with steady power
on your church, this day, this hour.
Raise, renew the life we've lost,
Spirit God of Pentecost.[1]

PRAYER PRACTICE

Put up your sail as you enter Centering Prayer, allowing the Spirit of God to blow in you, bringing refreshing breezes and giving you new life.

Read John 3:5–8. Be attentive to the ways the Spirit is moving you. Let a word of this scripture text indicate what that is. Pray that you may be responsive to the Spirit nudging you. Take a moment of silence to let that word guide you in your next step.

29 FIRE

> ...tongues, as of fire.
>
> —Acts 2:3

To rally enthusiasm for our football team the night before a game, students at my college gathered around a huge bonfire. There were speeches and music, but the fire itself transmitted a contagious energy, supporting the effort needed to win the battle of the morrow.

A roaring fire displays a ferocious consumption of fuel. We feel both its warmth and its power. In a controlled environment, fire inspires. On a cold day I like the cozy warmth of a flame in the fireplace of my study.

We have seen the attraction of the burning bush for Moses. In scripture, wind and fire indicate God's presence and action. Fire serves the Creator's power, purifying and energizing.

On Easter the two disciples who lived in Emmaus remembered how their hearts burned within them as the stranger who joined them on the road had explained the scriptures. When they shared a meal with him, they recognized him as the risen Christ (Luke 24:30-31). They quickly went back to Jerusalem to share the excitement of having seen the living Christ.

On the high festival day of Pentecost, as the disciples were gathered, waiting for the promised baptism of the Holy Spirit, tongues of fire appeared over each of them. These flames represented the presence and power of the Holy Spirit. The disciples were being empowered to take up the commission of bringing the gospel to Jerusalem, Judea, Samaria, and the rest of the world.

Fire was the word that best described the experience for Blaise Pascal, French mathematician and scientist, when he met Christ. On November 23, 1654, Pascal received a profound spiritual experience. Because he wanted always to remember and be inspired by that experience, he sewed a piece of paper into the lining of his coat. On the paper was written:

FIRE.
God of Abraham, God of Isaac, God of Jacob, not of the
philosophers and scholars.
Certitude. Certitude. Feeling. Joy. Peace.

God of Jesus Christ . . .
Joy, joy, joy, tears of joy.[1]

John of the Cross wrote about the fire of love that burns as a living flame in the soul.[2] He said, "For contemplation is naught else than a secret, peaceful and loving infusion from God, which, if it be permitted, enkindles the soul with the spirit of love."[3]

For all of fire's benefits, we take care with fire because it can be destructive. A purging fire destroys what needs to go. In Handel's great work *Messiah*, a soloist sings, "for he is like a refiner's fire." And the chorus responds, "and he shall purify." The fire of God burns away the sin of the world in preparation for the coming of Christ, ready to hear the "good tidings" and to "behold the glory of the Lord." The Spirit burning in us purges and empowers us.

Fire also warms. Living in a cold climate like Michigan's, I appreciate a fire's warmth. Our furnace runs from October to May. My wife and I can be comfortable in our home and heated buildings even in the cold of winter.

And within each of us, the fire of Christ can burn with compassion and generosity. Our spirit can be kindled by the flame of the Spirit. Like the spark plug in a car's engine, the spark of Christ can set a heart on fire. A deep longing for God can grow into a burning desire to love and serve the Lord.

I don't cause the fire in our fireplace to burn, but I can stoke the fire to get more oxygen to it. A bellows helps. The fire of Christ burning in me can be fanned by my practices of prayer and worship. Breathing in Christ through Centering Prayer, scripture reading, and gathering with other people of faith, all ignite the inner flame of the Spirit.

Stanzas 2 and 3 of the hymn "Wind Who Makes All Winds that Blow" by Thomas H. Troeger describes the fire of the Spirit:

Fire who fuels all fires that burn—
suns around which planets turn,
beacons marking reefs and shoals,
shining truth to guide our souls—
come to us as once you came:
burst in tongues of sacred flame!
Light and Power, Might and Strength,
fill your church, its breadth and length.

Holy Spirit, Wind and Flame,
move within our mortal frame.
Make our hearts an altar pyre.
Kindle them with your own fire.
Breathe and blow upon that blaze
till our lives, our deeds and ways
speak that tongue which every land
by your grace shall understand.[4]

PRAYER PRACTICE

Take time for Centering Prayer, giving consent to the fire of the Spirit's presence in you burning away what is harmful and building the warmth of love within you.

Read Acts 2:1-4. Consider how the Spirit of Christ ignited the spirits of the disciples on Pentecost and how the Spirit wants to kindle the fire of love in you. Listen to what God is saying to you. Pray for guidance and courage as you allow yourself to be transformed. Feel the fire of the Spirit burning in you.

CHRIST WITHOUT

30 DISCERNMENT

> . . . wisdom and discernment.
>
> —Deuteronomy 4:6

As I receive the gift of union with Christ, I am given a consciousness of the triune God in each moment. I am aware of God who is Creator, Redeemer, and Presence. I open myself to the guidance of the Spirit for decisions and inclinations. Breathing in the love of God and letting go of my ego, I come to the place of giving the divine love I have received. I need guidance in how best to be a participant in the divine work, so I pray for the leading of the Spirit. Here are some of the lessons I have learned about discernment:

1. *Discernment begins with prayer.* I ask the Holy Spirit to use my intuition as an instrument of divine guidance. The faculty called "intuition" can operate under the self's control, leading me to pursue pleasure; or it can be under the control of Christ as I turn my life over to him. When I yield to Christ, the Holy Spirit can prompt me to right thinking and action.

2. *Being clear about the nature of the decision is critical.* Sometimes I need help with this one. The Quakers have a custom of calling together a "clearness committee" when someone faces a significant decision. The committee of trusted people listens well and helps clarify what needs to be decided. Echoing this procedure, I often ask people I trust to listen to my situation and help me see it clearly. I can talk to someone who will listen and enlist that person's ears to hear and eyes to see the question I am facing. My spiritual director also will assist me in recognizing my options. I need to see as clearly as possible the alternatives that lie before me.

3. *The scriptures offer direction.* Principles from the Bible can point me toward a decision, and there are several ways to find relevant passages. A concordance and a Bible commentary help me search out key words, phrases, and passages relevant to my issues. I can also talk to a knowledgeable individual about what texts especially speak to aspects of my decision. By reading and meditating on such relevant scriptures, I'm able to apply biblical principles to my decision making.

4. *A list of the pros and cons for each possible road ahead is a useful tool.* This is a trick my mother taught me. She encouraged me to make a list of all the positives about a certain action and make another list of all the negatives. Then I could look at these lists to determine which outweighed the other. Later I learned that Ignatius had much to say about this method of making a decision. As a young man he chose between being a knight or a saint. Some years later he wrote about that decision and drew some conclusions for discernment. He said that creating a list of the positives and negatives about each alternative can help one determine which is God's direction. Ignatius encouraged attentiveness to feelings of consolation or desolation regarding each alternative. As I look at each alternative, I can imagine the best-case scenario and the worst-case scenario for each way.

5. *Consider whether the best outcome for a path fits with God's yearning or selfish desires.* I ask myself, *How can I express God's love in this world?* I also look at what I have to give up in order to follow a possible path: is it something important or something I need to let go of in order to follow God's will?

6. *After all this weighing, it's time for a decision.* I settle on a way to go. I make the decision in my own mind, tell others about it, and begin a course of action. I may take these steps without complete certainty, but I need to take a path, following the one that seems best at the moment and trusting God will make corrections.

7. *If it is of the Spirit, a decision will be ratified with inner peace.* It will feel good. In my experience, I often have second thoughts. Then I have to weigh these. Often they come from a lack of courage: I've let negatives in the path ahead loom large. There is never a perfect decision, because we live in an imperfect world. If the decision proves to be a poor one, there may be ways to reverse it or change course. But the second thoughts usually dissipate, and I move ahead with a sense of peace.

Sink in to the natural movement of breathing. Let your body take its natural course of inhaling and exhaling. There is nothing you need to decide or consciously command; breathing just happens. Now imagine yourself surrendering just as completely to the Spirit. Pray that you may take this attitude with you, allowing the Spirit to guide you in each moment, in each decision.

PRAYER PRACTICE

Take time for Centering Prayer, putting yourself in the hands of God.

Read Deuteronomy 4:5–8. Listen for the word the Holy Spirit gives you. Meditate on that word. Pray that the "statutes and ordinances" God gives will define the divine love by which you are guided. Be open in mind and heart to the inner prompting of the Spirit.

31 INTERCESSION

I urge that . . . intercessions . . . be made.

—1 Timothy 2:1

Spiritual breathing—receiving the love of God and letting go of obstacles to union with God—leads to sharing love with others. When the self-emptying love of God, as seen in Christ, shapes my attitude, I move toward being a person who self-lessly cares for others. Intercessory prayer flows from that caring.

As a contemplative, should I make my requests known to God or be content with whatever comes to me in God's good time? United in Christ to God, I become a participant in the work of God. When I specify my concerns in intercessory prayer, my petitions are part of life in God and God in me. As God acts in love I can be a partner in what happens. In divine providence every little movement contributes to the whole. My hopes and dreams originate in God. My concerns concern God, because God is All and in all. But this does not mean that God becomes my servant.

I may not get what I want, no matter how hard I pray, and no matter how many people have joined me in the same petition. I could not have prayed harder, nor can I imagine more people lifting the same prayer as I asked God to spare the life of my daughter-in-law when she was ill with a bacterial infection. Yet my request was not granted. Providence continued; divine love still embraced me. But she left us physically; I have to accept this tragic event. I cannot command God. I can only act as I am empowered and loved by our triune God.

This resonance with divine love springs forth in words of prayer: praise, thanksgiving, confession, supplication, and intercession. In our verbal prayers we ask that God's will be done in us and through us. We cooperate with the will of God in intercession for people and situations. We bring our specific requests with the desire that the divine will be done. We give voice to the desires that the Holy Spirit puts in us as best we can discern what to pray for. The Spirit prompts us, according to Romans 8:26: "We do not know how to pray as we ought, but that very Spirit intercedes with sighs too deep for words." Then we do what we are invited to do to participate in that divine will.

Invited to be participants in providence, we exercise our creativity along with the Creator. Human beings care for the earth, cultivating the garden of this world. God depends on our cooperation and creativity. God authors the smallest detail of our daily living, in our innermost spaces, in every life-giving breath. In the love we have received, we extend our love.

With Christ we can participate in the struggle for good over evil. Jesus came to enter human life, even unto death, to lift us to new life. His resurrection was the great triumph in history of love over hatred. As disciples we partake in his work of salvation. We seek healing and restoration. Verbally we lift our petitions for healing, peace, and justice. We blend our petitions with those of Christ who intercedes for us. Hebrews 7:24-25 says Christ, our high priest, "always lives to make intercession" for those who approach God through him. He is the suffering servant who "poured out himself to death, . . . and made intercession for the transgressors" (Isa. 53:12). As followers of Christ we pray for the salvation of the world.

I remember a conversation I had with a woman after the funeral of her mother, who had lived to an old age. The family had grown to the point where her mother had numerous grandchildren and great-grandchildren. She said, "I know that mother prayed for each of us every day. I believe her intercession was a means of blessing for us all. I now feel called to take up that ministry. I believe God is calling me to continue to pray for each member of our family daily." Perhaps you too have felt called to the ministry of intercession.

I have a long list of people I bring before God each day. I hold each person before God. Sometimes a specific request comes to me; sometimes I simply ask that God will bless that person. I'm not telling God what I think best for someone. I bring a person or situation before God, giving voice to the prayer the Holy Spirit gives me regarding that person or situation. When I intercede, I need to be ready to be part of the answer as God leads me.

These guidelines prepare the way for meaningful intercessory prayer:

1. Hold the person or situation in the light of God's love.

2. Ask God, *What is your desire for this person or situation?*

3. With the Holy Spirit as the author, express your request to God.

4. Be persistent.

5. Pray with confident hope.

6. Ask, *Is there anything I need to do for the person or situation?*

Now, sitting with eyes closed, let a person or a problem come to mind. Ask God, *What is your prayer for this person or this problem?* Raise that plea. Ask, *Is there anything I should do for this person or to help with this problem?* If you are called to do something, decide on your first step and move in that direction. Hold the person or problem for which you are praying in love. Ask that the will of God be done.

PRAYER PRACTICE

Take time for Centering Prayer, simply being in communion with God.

Read 1 Timothy 2:1-7. What stands out for you as you read these instructions for prayer? Take time to reflect on what intercessions you are called to offer. Pray for divine help in the ways of intercession to which you are called. In silence let the motivation you need grow in you.

32 ATTITUDE CHANGE

> . . . compassion, kindness, humility, meekness, and patience.
> —Colossians 3:12

A cartoon depicts a boy walking up the stairs. His mother asks, "Where are you going?" The boy replies, "I'm going up to my room to change my attitude."

Contemplative prayer changes our attitudes. When we go into Centering Prayer, we consent to God's presence and work within. Aware of divine love given to us, we can open ourselves to move away from old attitudes of resentment, superiority, inferiority, bitterness, and indifference toward new attitudes. We release preoccupations, let the love of God take hold, and allow Christ to change us. The calm increases patience and understanding, submerging judgmental attitudes. The acceptance we perceive dispels annoyance over things that don't go as we might like. Trust transforms fear. Time in Centering Prayer makes us a little more ready to be a calming presence for others. Regular practice grows attitudes of love, joy, peace, and patience.

The prayer closet is a good place for changing attitudes. There we put on the attitudes of Christ. Paul told the Colossians to put on a new suit of clothing, a new attitude. They were told to wear compassion, kindness, humility, meekness, and patience (Col. 3:12)—a remarkable wardrobe. In compassion we empathize with others. With kindness we notice how we can help. In humility we offer our service. In meekness we appreciate others rather than exalt ourselves. With patience we do not rush to get what we want. We move in concert with providence. As someone else has said, we move with the "pace of grace." "Above all," Paul said, "clothe yourselves with love, which binds everything together in perfect harmony" (Col. 3:14). The outfit coming from the change made in our prayer closet primarily expresses self-emptying love. We have thrown in the wash any bitterness, resentment, coldness, callousness, isolation, and fear that we might have worn. We have left hanging what might be pretentious, exerting self over others. We have discarded suggestions of power. We have chosen bright colors of cheer that will encourage. We put on garments that invite trust and hope. We have accented that we care.

When we go to a party we want to dress appropriately. What we wear says a lot about us and about our opinion of the event. Clothing can express respect for the people we meet. To follow Paul's advice, we want to show regard for the people we meet. Being too formally dressed might say we are cool toward them. Being too casually dressed might say we don't care much about them. As careful as we are about physical dress, Paul suggests we also might be concerned about spiritual attitudes and how we carry them.

We can give people warmth and care. We can express our regard for them with a smile, a handshake, and a hug where appropriate. We can be good listeners, present in a way that invites the other to unload pain and pressure. We can take the time to hear what people have to say, responding with open questions. We can refrain from telling how we know because we have been there. Instead of rushing to say something about ourselves, we can absorb what is being said. We can convey genuine concern and offer encouragement by sharing the other's emotions and feelings. We can avoid trying to repair, fix, or explain. Attentive listening encourages hurting people to talk, because it expresses a caring presence. Clothed with the love of Christ, we become loving listeners. We reflect the feelings of another with sympathetic silence, with encouraging words, empathetic sadness, or a smile or even laughter. We become the means of Christ's blessing.

Let your spiritual attitude be like breathing: inhaling and exhaling, receiving and giving. Breathe in love; breathe out antagonism. Breathe in acceptance; breathe out bitterness. Breathe in humility; breathe out judgment. Breathe in the Spirit; breathe out selfishness.

PRAYER PRACTICE

Sit quietly in Centering Prayer to let the Spirit work in you, giving you a change of attitude.

Read Colossians 3:12-17. Listen for what God is saying to you about your attitudes. Where is change needed? How can you allow the Holy Spirit to make the change you need? Pray for that transformation. Going forward take with you the change that you have heard God wanting to make in you.

33 COMMUNITY

All who believed were together.

—Acts 2:44

We were literally "surrounded by such a great cloud of witnesses" (NIV). With origins going back to 1703, First Reformed Church was the oldest organization in New Brunswick, New Jersey. Just like the churches in Europe, it was surrounded by a cemetery, in which many founders of the Reformed Church in America, the City of New Brunswick, and Rutgers University were buried. The congregation I was serving had a great time each fall with a "living history" storytelling. In period costume, we stood by the gravesites of these significant people and told their stories. I enacted the third pastor of the church, who also was the first president of Queens College, later to become Rutgers University. The people we remembered came alive to us. We were inspired by their stories, even as the author of Hebrews felt encouraged by the host of heaven who witnessed the race now being run (Heb. 12:1).

The community of which we are a part includes those who have preceded us in death as well as those who are beside us in the walk with God. I like the idea of Celtic Christians that our deceased loved ones are not far away. Only a thin membrane separates us. They give us their love and care from their place of union with God.

A request came to me as pastor of the First Reformed Church. A member of the church asked for a room to hold a weekly meeting devoted to developing friendships. It would be a time and place where people could get to know one another. The necessary permission was granted, but I wondered why the church was not already addressing this need. It grieved me that the church had so missed its calling to become an intimate community.

We are one body in Christ. Baptism signifies our union with Christ, and in the Lord's Supper we receive the indwelling Presence. In sacraments and life together, the church expresses the "communion of the saints." Perhaps some people who have vowed to live a communal life take this very seriously. Many of us treasure our individualism. We know that differentiation is important to personal growth, and we want to be as independent as possible. Yet we have in us the desire for community. Howard Thurman, a poet and mystic of the twentieth century, said, "To be in unity with the Spirit is to be in unity with one's fellows."[1]

A congregation is made up of many disparate people, with a variety of opinions. They find a common identity in Christ, which frees them from power struggles and anxiety over differences. Even if a minority of people in a congregation take time for contemplative prayer, their nonanxious presence will have a profound effect. Their deep relationship with God will affect relationships throughout the community. Walls of separation between people are broken down; "Christ is all and in all!" (Col. 3:11).

The Church of the Servant in Grand Rapids, Michigan, surrounded our family with love when my daughter-in-law, Karen, died. We felt the wonderful support of the community. For the next two years, people of the congregation remembered Karen on the anniversary of her death. They expressed their sympathy in words, notes, and hugs. One member led a service of remembrance in the chapel on the anniversary, with prayers from the Book of Common Prayer and spontaneous prayers.

Community grows among us from the intimacy of love shared by the three persons of the Holy Trinity. That love provides our true home. In the love of Christ we are united with those living and dead. Through the incarnation we are made partakers in the divine community of eternal love.

In Centering Prayer we enter that union with the triune God. And the practice deepens our sense of oneness with the whole human family. We participate in union with Christ. In that communion of prayer we are drawn into community. Writing about community, Timothy Koock, a longtime practitioner of Centering Prayer and a former trustee of Contemplative Outreach, says, "Communion is the grace which flows within a community and gives it Life."[2] Thomas R. Ward, Episcopal priest and leader of Centering Prayer retreats, writes, "In Centering Prayer we enter into intimacy with one another through intimacy with God."[3] The booklet *Community: Oneness in Contemplation* of the Contemplative Life Program explains:

> Out of the silence of contemplative prayer comes the awareness that we are part of a greater whole. As Meister Eckhart suggests, ones who are wholly surrounded by the presence of God, enveloped by God, clothed with God, in oneness with God—such ones have a common meeting point with one another.[4]

The contemplative community becomes sensitive to the needs of others, wanting to express compassion. This communion "has a welcoming quality to it, like the special way one received an honored guest or loved one into one's home."[5] With selfless giving we put the good of others ahead of our own. With hospitality we build community. Dorothy Day made room for the poor and the afflicted because, she said, "They are Christ."[6] We are told in Romans 12:13: "Contribute to the needs of the saints; extend hospitality to strangers." As God has welcomed us in Christ so we welcome one another to be at home with us in God.

PRAYER PRACTICE

As you inhale, be thankful for all the people who have helped you. As you exhale, resolve anew to do all you can to build community. In Centering Prayer be aware that you sit with a vast community of people in prayer.

Read Acts 2:43–47. Note the characteristics of the first Christian community. Let a word from the reading speak to you. Ask God what that word means for you. Pray for divine assistance. Let the word shape your participation in community.

34 Church

"I have sent them into the world."

—John 17:18

They weren't so far off, I thought to myself. I had strived to motivate the first church I served as pastor to become a change agent for social action. The church in Pottersville, New Jersey, features a picturesque Christmas card–style sanctuary in a valley of the Somerset Hills. Later, serving an inner city church in Union City, New Jersey, I worked to help congregants recognize the mission they had to the city. But over time, I began to appreciate that the church exists first of all for worship. The people of the Pottersville church knew this. Their first loyalty was to gather for worship.

The life of a church flows from worship. The people of a congregation become the body of Christ united with him and doing his work. John Calvin declared that in Holy Communion we enter "that intimate fellowship in which we are joined with his flesh."[1] Calvin said:

> Our souls are fed by the flesh and blood of Christ in the same way that bread and wine keep and sustain physical life. . . . Souls find their nourishment in Christ—which cannot happen unless Christ truly grows into one with us.[2]

In worship we gather to express love for God. Receiving divine love evokes praise and thanksgiving. In our liturgy we express gratitude and adoration: giving thanks for the gifts coming to us by the grace of God; giving ourselves to God in adoration; putting in words our appreciation of God's love in Christ; confessing our sin and our need for forgiveness and mercy. We pray for help in following the path that has become open to us. We pray for assistance in following the directions we have received for sharing divine love, and we make our petitions. In word and song we are expressing the love we have because God first loved us.

Intent on social change, I failed to appreciate how the people of the Pottersville church came together in response to the grace of God. The book of Psalms, the prayer book for people of faith over the last three thousand years, contains songs of thanksgiving, praise, and lament. In five "books," corresponding with the five books of the Torah, the Psalms respond to what God has done. In similar fashion, worship with liturgies of gathering, listening to the Word, celebrating around a table, and sending forth into the world, responds to the grace of the Trinity.

I have come to see that we can express this love of God in a variety of ways. In the Western church words are primary in worship. In the Eastern church visual images play a larger role. And in contemplation we offer adoration in silent communion with God.

Worship comes first, as the people in Pottersville recognized, but mission flows from this worship of God. In worship the gathered community demonstrates the love of Christ. After Peter denied his Lord three times, the risen Christ confronted him with the question, "Do you love me?" As Peter said indeed he did, Jesus asked him to feed his sheep (John 21:15-17). Followers of Jesus are called to tend the flock of faith with care and nurture. Too often churches have not been able to display unity, but, at least at times, the people assembled as "church" have practiced divine love. Jesus summarized all that the law and the prophets had said in the words: "'You shall love the LORD your God with all your heart, and with all your soul, and with all your mind.' This is the greatest and first commandment. And a second is like it: 'You shall love your neighbor as yourself'" (Matt. 22:37-39). The church demonstrates this love, grown in worship, as adoration of our triune God— our Source, Word, and Spirit. The worshiping community loves the Source of our being with gratitude. The community of faith loves the Redeemer with appreciation of our forgiveness. The church loves the Holy Spirit as it makes space for Divine Presence and power.

As we participate in the love of God, we naturally share divine love in the world. The church proclaims the good news of the kingdom to persons who need salvation and to nations that need transformation. By sharing the love of God, the church fulfills Jesus' prayer to his Father that "the love with which you have loved me may be in them, and I in them" (John 17:26). The church proclaims the gospel to the oppressed, diseased, and imprisoned. Jesus called on his group of followers to communicate the good news of the kingdom of God. The church does this in both word and action; in discussing one's own experience of God and helping people have the food and shelter they need. Jesus commissioned his disciples: "Go into all the world and proclaim the good news to the whole creation" (Mark 16:15). Attempting to follow that command, followers of Jesus have worked together in churches.

Sharing the good news of the kingdom often requires action. In action we express our love for God. In service to others we live with generosity, the way we have been graced by our divine Lover. Through the church we participate in many acts of compassion throughout the world.

With breathing in, silently repeat *Lord Jesus Christ*. With exhaling, *Guide me in sharing your grace and love.*

PRAYER PRACTICE

Enter into Centering Prayer knowing that you pray with a church extending throughout the world.

Read Matthew 22:34–40. Listen to Jesus' summary of all the law and the prophets. Take the word that resonates in you, pondering its meaning. Give thanks and praise in loving response. Pray for the church, its task of communicating the gospel in our world. Let the word you have received become your script for loving and serving the Lord.

35 PRAYING CONSTANTLY

Pray without ceasing.

—1 Thessalonians 5:17

One result of the daily discipline of contemplative prayer has surprised me. I thought the results would come during the prayer periods. I expected some good feelings to arise as I spent time in prayer, and some wonderful moments have been mine, but at times it all seems quite routine. The surprise came in a greater awareness of God at other times. I saw the handiwork of the Creator in the majestic shapes and beautiful colors of trees. I found the presence of Christ in the people I met. I realized the power of the Spirit in events that came together. My time in prayer prepared me to notice the Presence of God in each moment.

A regular practice of prayer leads to a constant attitude of prayer, an awareness of God in every moment of the day. This doesn't mean constantly thinking of words to address the Holy One. Sometimes it means silence. Remember the multidimensional aspects of prayer. I talk, and I listen, and I silently commune with God. When I pray constantly, at every moment, I receive and give the love of God, participating in the divine delight in being. I know in each moment the Divine Presence in me and around me. I live in Christ and Christ in me as Jesus taught: "Abide in me as I abide in you" (John 15:4).

Paul wrote that he was constantly in prayer for the believers in Philippi. He remembered them; they were on his mind and heart, so he was "constantly praying with joy" for all of them. I find it interesting that he added the words "with joy." He did not pray as a duty-bound activity. Remembering people in Philippi gave him joy. Paul prayed for them as a delightful effort. It lifted his spirits.

In prayer we participate in the delight God takes in each of us. We make specific petitions for people as we become aware of their need. Holding them in the light of Christ, we ask for the Spirit to work in them.

I understand *praying without ceasing* as a consciousness of the presence of God in each moment. I have found an *active prayer*, also called a *breath prayer*, promotes this consciousness. I take a sentence with me throughout the day. Sometimes it comes into my consciousness; sometimes it lies below the surface. For some time, my breath prayer has been *Keep me aware of your presence.* Recently, because I sense I need more than presence, I am forming a prayer that says, *Lord Jesus Christ, keep me united with you.* By grace I am united with Christ in his incarnation, crucifixion, resurrection, and ascension. I receive and share the breath of God as the living Christ breathes in me. I am aware of something more than drawing air into my lungs and expelling carbon dioxide: the divine Spirit lives and breathes in me. I am blessed with gifts of life, and I am giving myself to life in every moment. I exist in that rhythm of receiving and giving.

Eastern Orthodox Christians breathe with the phrases of the Jesus Prayer. They pray *Lord Jesus Christ* as they inhale and *have mercy on me* as they exhale. The prayer creates a constant receiving of Christ's grace and a release of all that needs to fall away. *The Way of the Pilgrim* explains that this prayer becomes a constant internal refrain.

You can create a breath prayer by going deep within and translating your deepest longing into a short sentence. The Jesus Prayer may be the one you want to use. Or you may identify words of scripture that express your deep desire. There may be other words given to you that express the cutting edge of your longing to love and serve the Lord. Add to those words your favorite name of God and you have a prayer to take with you throughout the day.[1]

Take the time to form a breath prayer to take with you for the rest of the day. Recall it as you have moments of quiet. Let it become so much a part of your psyche that it springs up frequently.

PRAYER PRACTICE

In Centering Prayer let your breath bring you into a consciousness of God. Let go of thoughts to dwell in that awareness for twenty minutes.

Read Philippians 1:3-11. Let a word touch you within. Meditate on what that word says to you. What does it suggest for your daily walk with God? Ask God for support in following this suggestion. Be in silence with this prayer for a little while. Then take it with you as you go about your next activities.

36   Gratitude

Give thanks to the LORD.

—Psalm 107:1

I can easily be in an angry mood when things aren't going the way I want. Resentment builds up within me, then comes out in snide remarks. I can be upset that so much snow fell last night. This morning I had over a foot of snow in places to plow through with my snowblower. But instead of getting angry over the situation, I can be thankful that I have a snow-blower and the strength to operate it.

We all have a choice of being grateful or being annoyed—looking at the donut or the hole. Will we choose to notice body aches and pains, sad-ness of heart, difficulties we face? We can choose to see the good coming our way. With gratitude, we find much for which to be thankful. Consider the strategy in the old song: "Count your many blessings, name them one by one, And it will surprise you what the Lord hath done." We can be in the moment with expectancy and attentiveness, knowing God is there.

I have a habit of offering a brief prayer, *Thank you, God,* when good things happen. But all too often, pain and disappointment rob me of that custom. My attention to God needs renewal. In prayer I may express to God my laments, but thanksgiving will rescue me from bitter complaint.

The New Testament epistles admonish gratitude: living in Christ means "abounding in thanksgiving" (Col. 2:7). Scripture teaches us to "give thanks in all circumstances" (1 Thess. 5:18). In the strongest terms scripture instructs us to live carefully "giving thanks to God the Father at all times and for everything" (Eph. 5:20).

Still, that phrase *for everything* gives me some difficulty. Must I be thankful for the large snowfall? Am I to be thankful that my son-in-law died or for the infection that took my daughter-in-law's life or for the cancer that threatened my wife some years ago? Giving thanks for every-thing in all circumstances runs counter to my disposition. I tend to get angry, bitter, resentful. I need to bring to God my laments, my sadness. As gratitude reigns, I accept what happens and give thanks for the presence and action of God in the situation. Of course, God is there in each tragic event. Nothing can separate us from the love of God (Rom. 8:38-39).

Even in dire circumstances, I am loved and cared for by God. At these times when disaster struck, I took notice and saw that the providence of God continued. In the sense that even in these events much good continues, I can be grateful *for* them. And beyond that, I know that from the divine perspective, even events that seem the worst to me are known to God who loves me. After all, both joy and sadness fill every moment; that is the nature of human life. Ingredients of good and bad make up every experience. Knowing that enables me to be grateful for the whole gift of life, even the events I consider tragic.

In an attitude of contemplation we see God in all things, even crises. The gratitude by which we live includes giving thanks for specific gifts, and it becomes an attitude for life as we are grateful for the Giver in all that happens. The prophet Habakkuk expressed gratitude when things did not go his way:

> Though the fig tree does not blossom,
> and no fruit is on the vines;
> though the produce of the olive fails,
> and the fields yield no food;
> though the flock is cut off from the fold,
> and there is no herd in the stalls,
> yet I will rejoice in the LORD;
> I will exult in the God of my salvation. (Hab. 3:17-18)

The Eucharist can point the way to gratitude, because it celebrates both the death and the resurrection of Christ. The Resurrection reveals the ultimate result of all struggles. The grace of Christ binds us to the love of God.

At our first Thanksgiving meal without Karen, I gave thanks to God. I told the group at our table that I thank God for all Karen meant to us. She exemplified the fruit of the Spirit—gentleness, kindness, and faithfulness. I am thankful to God for all the blessings that came to us through her. This gratitude helps me realize the gift she is to many.

Five and a half years after my son-in-law's death and a year and half after my daughter-in-law's death, I end my morning stretch time at a doorway where I look across the hall to a collage of family photos. Recently, as I gazed on those photos, I felt gratitude for those two people who were so much a part of our family. I could thank God for all they were and all they have meant to us. Sadness remains, but it is tempered by thanksgiving. This thankfulness leads me to know that these loved ones, now with God, continue to love us and we, them.

I can live my life with gratitude for all God has done for me. Everything around me comes as gift. I live by grace, knowing this gratitude results. Karl Barth said, "Gratitude follows grace like thunder lightning."[1] Both grace and gratitude derive from the Latin word *gratia*, taking pleasure in a gift or relationship. A statement of faith in my tradition says that gratitude motivates my daily living; *The Heidelberg Catechism* says that all I do with my life can be an expression of gratitude. The catechism raises this question: since my salvation comes entirely as a gift of God, why try to live a good life? After all, nothing I can do earns divine favor. God's love comes as gift. I can live a holy life because of the "gratitude I owe to God for [my] redemption."[2] In response to God's grace I try to live in a way that expresses my thanks. *The Heidelberg Catechism* asks, "Why must we do good works?" and replies, "So that with our whole life we may show ourselves grateful to God."[3]

When gratitude becomes as natural as breathing, we become conscious of providence in every moment. We see the work of God, feel God's love, receive the gifts of the One who cares for us. We more readily release distress to the One who governs all; we let go of anger and anxiety and allow the love of God to flow through us. When thanksgiving becomes a habit, it increases our vision of Divine Presence and grace. As fear and anxiety diminish, we sense the providence of God and see signs of the beauty, truth, and goodness of God. We are healed of fear, insecurity, and resentment.

Now, as you inhale, let a blessing you are being given come to mind. As you exhale, give thanks with the words *I thank you, God.*

PRAYER PRACTICE

Take time for Centering Prayer with gratitude especially for the Giver, not (at this moment) for the gifts.

Read Colossians 3:15-17. Listen for the message God has for you about giving thanks. Meditate on the word you are given. Pray for divine help in practicing the gratitude scripture teaches. Take a moment of silence to set the tone of gratitude in this day.

37   One with I Am

"... that they may all be one."

—John 17:21

Certainly Jesus' prayer, as stated in John 17, was that all his followers will be in unity. Church divisions have been a terrible scandal. We must join Jesus in praying that they will be overcome.

But Jesus prayed for something even deeper. He asked that we may be one with God, even as he was one with the Father. We work so hard to find and build up ourselves. When we give ourselves to Christ, we make the ultimate surrender. We become united with Christ. We become participants in God. In this union we experience something of heaven on earth. Already now we experience the death of the false self and resurrection of the true self. The end of this earthly journey will bring transformation, the ultimate yielding of ourselves to be at home in God.

We live in God the way the little fish in the ocean who, not seeing it, asked, "Where is the ocean?" As Teresa of Ávila said, we don't need wings to search for God. We can humbly walk with God because God is with us.[1] God is closer than consciousness itself. Nothing in life or in death can separate us from the love of God (Rom. 8:38-39).

So I know that I am never alone; I exist in the whole of existence, part of a whole, one with all that is. Like a facet of a great chandelier, I am a crystal refracting the divine light present in all. I sparkle as I reflect the light of Christ. I do not exist alone but become one with the many who make this great cosmos of divine light. "I am" as I am in the great I Am.

How can we be both diverse and one at the same time? We see this mystery in the Trinity. God exists as three in one. We can be one with God and at the same time individual partakers and participants in the one being. We "may become participants of the divine nature" (2 Pet. 1:4). We are made in the likeness of God to participate in and embody the divine nature. Jesus prayed that his followers would be one in God, just as he and the Father existed in each other (John 17:21).

I like the way *The Heidelberg Catechism* puts it: "That I belong ... not to myself but to my faithful Savior, Jesus Christ."[2] Romans 14:8 tells us, "We are the Lord's," and 1 Corinthians 6:19-20 says, "You are not your own . . . you were bought with a price." I do not belong to myself; I belong to Christ.

With the practice of Centering Prayer we go deeper into our walk with God. We spend time with God in intimate communion but not as a solitary experience. In silent communion with God we participate in the divine concern for all creation. Far from an individualistic experience, Centering Prayer calls us to become aware of our unity with God and all of God's creation. Some consider piety a private matter, but Jesus calls us to realize our oneness with Christ and with all who share in his grace. Thomas Keating explains:

> One of the things that Centering Prayer, as it deepens, will affect is our intuition of the oneness of the human family, and indeed, the oneness of all creation. As one moves into one's own inmost being, one comes into contact with what is the inmost being of everyone else. Although each of us retains his or her own unique personhood, we are necessarily associated with the Divine-human person who has taken the whole human family to Himself in such a way as to be the inmost reality of each individual member of it.[3]

With our Western thinking we regard our environment as "other"; actually, it is more like our mother. The air we breathe comes from the plants of the earth. This air has been circulating around the world for a long time. It contains particles that have been breathed by animals and humans throughout history. The molecules you inhale could have been in the lungs of Jesus or Mary, Peter or Paul or Mary Magdelene. All life on earth shares one breath. Air is used and reused through the years, giving life to each generation. With the air we breathe we are united with people of every era and place.

As we live in one Lord, by one faith, with one baptism, we are united with God and neighbor and all creation. We live in God and God in us. We live in that faith. God says, "Do not fear, for I am with you" (Isa. 41:10), and Jesus says, "I am with you always, to the end of the age" (Matt. 28:20).

I may not know that I am united with God because of obstacles to that union. I may refuse the love offered to me. But, in fact, "I am" because I am united with the great I AM.

Breathe ten conscious breaths, imagining with each one a person or creature who might have once breathed the air you now breathe. Choose people from different eras or places. Be aware of the unity we enjoy with all creatures.

PRAYER PRACTICE

In a time of Centering Prayer be open to receive the immediate presence of God. Know that we are one with divinity and divinity with us.

Read John 17:20-23. Let the word God wants to give you shine in this passage. Take time to reflect on the difference it makes for you. Pray that what you are being given becomes an integral part of your life. Be grateful for the oneness you have with God.

38 CRUCIFIED

Our old self was crucified with him.

—Romans 6:6

Visual images help me to see God. I know the inadequacy of any mental image I might have of the Divine. The unseen and unknowable can be known to us only in a relationship of love. Mental constructs cannot fathom God. Yet I am human and need some symbols to help me. The book *The Shack* creates a warm and inviting picture of the Trinity. So it appeals to those whose previous view of God was too harsh.

For a likeness of God I look at Jesus. I see this master teacher on his knees, washing his disciples feet. He acts as a servant, bending down, cleansing the feet of the disciples who have walked dusty roads and accumulated dirt on their feet. With cooling water and a dry towel he refreshes them. I see this man of compassion praying in the garden of Gethsemane, asking that he may be spared the suffering to which his life has led, but accepting the will of his Father. His agony results from our rebellion against God. He willingly accepts humiliation and unspeakable pain for the sake of his sisters and brothers. I see him appearing to his disciples after his death with wounds on his hands and side. Forever he bears the pain of our selfishness, so that we may be made whole.

In this picture I see God and how I can be an image of God. Like Jesus, I am to give myself in love of God. Paul spoke of his being crucified with Christ so the risen Christ lived in him. What self Paul had was not held, hoarded, or possessed but given away. He said, "I have been crucified with Christ; and it is no longer I who live, but it is Christ who lives in me" (Gal. 2:19-20).

Like Christ, I am crucified. I let myself, with my ambitions and desires, die. I become a servant. I accept loss. My ego diminishes. I lose interest in advancing my own name. As the Spirit reforms me to be like Jesus, I live in the likeness of God. When Jesus said, "Take up [your] cross," he meant be ready to die (Matt. 16:24). Carrying a cross signified going to one's execution. In the first century, and still today in some places, being a follower of Christ can mean death. And there is a broader meaning in what Jesus asks of us. The old self dies when we accept new life in Christ. This letting go runs counter to the strongest of all instincts. Naturally we want to preserve our lives, not give up ourselves and be totally identified with Christ. This requires a conversion, a transformation, leaving the selfish life to become unified with God.

We visited Karen's grave on December 23, to express our love in a Christmas filled with sadness. My wife, son, his three children, and I went to place a wreath on the grave. In my reflection I wondered what had happened to the blanket of love covering Karen that I saw when she lay ill in the hospital. Was it gone, absolved in the cold? Or was it still surrounding her, represented by the snow now, and real in another realm? The grave reminds us of her, now united with God, embraced in love, in a blanket forever lasting. After all, Christmas celebrates the coming of Immanuel, God with us. Divine love enfolds us eternally. We enter that realm as we surrender totally to God. John Wesley wrote:

> Be patterns to all, of denying yourselves, and taking up your cross daily. Let them see that you make no account of any pleasure which does not bring you nearer to God, nor regard any pain which does; that you simply aim at pleasing him, whether by doing or suffering; that the constant language of your heart, with regard to pleasure or pain, honour or dishonour, riches or poverty, is, 'All's alike to me, so I in my Lord may live and die!'[1]

Wesley's words remind me to let go. I sing, "I surrender all. All to Jesus I surrender." Crucifixion does not mean I kill the old self. I can't do that. My attachments to money, sex, and power are too great. The false self works to strengthen those attachments. The old self dies as I let go and accept the transforming work of Christ. He frees me from the old self and raises me to a new life. I yield to his work in me.

Breathing deeply, know that you are united with Christ in his death and resurrection. Let go of the desires of the false self so you may represent the love and joy of Christ.

PRAYER PRACTICE

Be in Centering Prayer, surrendering all to Jesus.

Read Romans 6:5-11. Meditate on the word that stands out for you, asking what God is saying. Release attachments and self-identification to surrender to Christ. Let a moment of silence deepen that detachment.

39   Dry Bones Breathed into Life

"Breathe upon these slain, that they may live."
—Ezekiel 37:9

I am helpless. I don't want to think that way, because I like to believe I am in control, with the power to do what I want. So I fool myself. In reality, I live only because I am given the gift of life. I have meaning only because I can be an instrument of divine love. I have the power to do what I am called to do only because the Holy Spirit empowers me. I am dead in "trespasses and sins" (Eph. 2:1) unless given life in Christ.

In a vision, Ezekiel sees a valley of dry, old bones. Everywhere he looks he sees death. The Spirit questions Ezekiel, "Can these bones live?" The prophet replies, "Lord God, you know." Then the Spirit tells Ezekiel to speak to the bones,

> "O dry bones, hear the word of the Lord. . . . I will cause breath to enter you, and you shall live. I will lay sinews on you, and will cause flesh to come upon you, and cover you with skin, and put breath in you, and you shall live; and you shall know that I am the Lord." (Ezek. 37:4-6)

When Ezekiel speaks to the bones, a great noise of rattling bones coming together rises in the valley; sinews and flesh and skin appear. The Spirit tells Ezekiel to say more, "Prophesy to the breath, prophesy, mortal, and say to the breath: Thus says the Lord God: Come from the four winds, O breath, and breathe upon these slain, that they may life" (Ezek. 37:9). And as he speaks again a vast multitude of live people fill the valley. The Spirit tells Ezekiel that the dry bones represent the people of Israel. As he prophesies to them God will bring them back to life. The divine Spirit will restore them.

Without the breath of the Spirit, we too are dry bones, helpless. But by grace, the Wind blows, breathing life into us. When we receive the breath of God, we are given new life. With Christ we are raised to life in God and with God. As Jesus died on the cross and was raised, so the Spirit of God gives us resurrection with him.

We are promised this resurrection power through Christ. God reigns, giving life in Christ, "so that God may be all in all" (1 Cor. 15:28). Paul wrote to the Romans about how we are resurrected in Christ. He said that God who raised Christ from the dead will "give life to your mortal bodies also through his Spirit that dwells in you" (Rom. 8:11).

Raised with Christ we become part of a new order, the kingdom of God. The breath of God shapes our lives. Our dry bones come alive, uniting us in the body of Christ; we find ourselves in a new community. As we discern the way God works, we see how we can participate in the building of the kingdom. We do not build the kingdom; God does that. We become participants in the kingdom and citizens of it. As such, we work for peace in our world; we work to establish justice, and we join in the care of the earth.

My dry bones gain life when I witness the light and love of God. A neighbor across the street places a large illuminated angel in her bay window during the Christmas season. That angel symbolizes hope for me when I look out on a dark, cold night and see its radiance. When I breathe deep of the joy and hope the angel represents, the long winter night's heavy gloom of sadness is lifted.

Let the breath of God fill your being. Give all of yourself to being a person of love as you exhale the love God has for you.

The more we pray, the more old forms fall away: prayer time becomes formless. Prayer is nothing more or less than an awareness of the love of God. It becomes a rehearsal for consciousness of God in every moment. Verbal prayers and Bible study continue to have their place, but in the silence of Centering Prayer we simply enjoy being in the mysterious presence of God, and God in us. By taking this time, our lives will be shaped with a new awareness of God. And we will be people of compassion.

Twice a day I let the breath of God enliven my dry bones. I sit in Centering Prayer, letting the love of God flow into me. The challenges of each day, the discouragements that come, can dry me out. I need the replenishment of Centering Prayer. Renewed, I can go out with energy to be the person I am called to be.

Stand erect, as tall as possible. Visualize the bones of your skeleton that give structure to your body: begin with the bones of your feet and slowly move upward to your cranium. Imagine the tissue that holds these bones together to be infused with the life of the Holy Spirit. Feel the Spirit coursing through your body.

PRAYER PRACTICE

Take time for Centering Prayer to allow the breath of the Spirit to flow within you.

Read Ezekiel 37:1-14. What is the word you most need to hear from this text? Open yourself to the inflowing Spirit, restoring and empowering you. Pray that you will keep breathing in the gifts of God and breathing out the love of God. Let the resurrection power of the Spirit give you a consciousness of God in your next activities.

40 CHRIST BREATHED THE SPIRIT

He breathed on them.

—John 20:22

The risen Christ, God with us, breathed his Spirit into the disciples. On Sunday, after Jesus was crucified on Friday, the living Christ stood among the gathered disciples and said, "Peace be with you. As the Father has sent me, so I send you" (John 20:21). Then he breathed on the disciples, saying, "Receive the Holy Spirit" (John 20:22).

Christ breathed on them. The disciples were steeped in scripture and knew well the story of God breathing life into Adam and Ezekiel's vision that the breath of God can resurrect a valley of dry bones. They realized that Jesus was giving them the Spirit to guide and empower them. In the act of breathing, Christ bestowed the power that would be their source of strength as they engaged in the work of Christ. That power became manifest at Pentecost when the disciples were filled with the Holy Spirit and as Peter spoke of the resurrection of Christ, being "exalted at the right hand of God, and having received from the Father the promise of the Holy Spirit, he has poured out this that you both see and hear" (Acts 2:33).

The living Christ, Jesus resurrected—guiding the church from the right hand of God and present with every receiver—breathes the Holy Spirit into us. We receive that breath/Spirit of God as we consent to the presence and action of God in us. This gift comes to each of us in different ways.

We may receive the presence and power of the risen Christ when we know God loves us. This happened to Mary Magdalene as she grieved at the tomb of Jesus. When he tenderly spoke her name, she knew him. Before that she thought he was the gardener. When it became clear that he knew her intimately, she recognized him. Then Jesus told her to let go, not cling to him, but to go tell others (John 20:11-18).

We may receive the presence and power of the risen Christ as did the two walking from Jerusalem to Emmaus. A stranger joined them, imparting a new understanding of scripture and a burning heart. Then, in the breaking of bread, they realized Christ's presence. We know in the Eucharist that he lives in us. And becoming so aware, we go back to our Jerusalem to share the good news (Luke 24:13-35).

Or we may receive the presence and power of the risen Christ in a state of doubt when friends persuade us to meet with them in a faith community. We may feel like Thomas, who said, "Unless I see the mark of the nails in his hands and put my finger in the mark of the nails and my hand in his side, I will not believe." There, in the community, the risen Christ invites us to touch and feel and know what he suffered in love for us. This gift explodes in praise, "My Lord and my God!" (John 20:24-29).

We may receive the presence and power of the risen Christ as we are at our usual work. Peter went back to fishing. In the one who appeared on the beach and provided a miraculous catch of fish, he knew the resurrected Jesus. Three times Jesus asked him, "Do you love me?" Three times Peter affirmed his love and was called to exercise that love in nurturing others (John 21:1-19).

We may receive the presence and power of the risen Christ as we help someone in need. We give a drink of water, visit someone who is ill, or help serve a meal, and we realize the one we are serving is Christ (Matt. 25:31-46).

We may receive the presence and power of the risen Christ as we champion a cause in which we believe. Suddenly we're given new vision. Paul was on his way to persecute Christians in the belief that his law-bound way was right. His view changed entirely when he encountered the risen Christ. His personal acquaintance with Christ set his life on a new course of service (Acts 9:1-22).

Or we may receive the presence and power of the risen Christ as we huddle with others in fear. The living Christ breaks in and sends us forth with a breath of new life. Each person's experience will be unique. But Christ touches us and tugs us and transforms us to receive him with love and devotion. The empowerment of the Spirit of Christ will move us to be witnesses of the risen Christ and to testify to all we can reach.

I receive the gift of the Spirit as I realize that Christ is breathing on me, empowering me to be a little Christ. In the joyful gift of breathing I participate in the gift of life. There will be a day when that physical breathing stops. Then I still will be held in the love of God, the risen Christ breathing on me. I surrender as the Spirit moves in every moment. Christ becomes my all in all. Receiving and giving, filled and emptied, in gains and in losses, I am embraced in the love of God. As I am filled with the breath of Christ I experience and re-present the incarnation, God with us.

The rhythm of life consists of receiving and giving. We receive the gift of life and give in turn. We receive the revelation of God and give of ourselves in return. We do that every time we breath, physically and spiritually.

The love of our Source, Eternal Word, and Holy Spirit fills the atmosphere as surely as the air we breathe. Breathe deep. Be filled with that love and surrender to the mystery of the moment.

PRAYER PRACTICE

Take time for Centering Prayer, consenting to the breath of Christ which gives you life.

Read John 20:19-23. Ask God to speak to you through this story of Jesus' resurrection. Picture Christ breathing on you. Imagine him filling you with his Spirit. Meditate on what receiving that gift means for you. Pray that the Spirit of Christ may guide and empower you for whatever way Christ calls you to be and to serve this day. Be in silence for a moment with gratitude for the power of God at work in your life and the ways you are able to share the love of God.

"Let everything that breathes praise the LORD!"

—Psalm 150:6

This page constitutes a continuation of the copyright page.

NOTES

INTRODUCTION

1. *Calvin: Institutes of the Christian Religion*, ed. John T. McNeill, trans. Ford Lewis Battles, vol. 20 (Philadelphia, PA: Westminster Press, 1960), 737.

2. John Calvin, *Calvin's Commentaries: Isaiah*, trans. John King (Grand Rapids, MI: Baker Book House, 1981), 3:635.

3. John Calvin, *Calvin's Commentaries: The Epistles of Paul the Apostle to the Galatians, Ephesians, Philippians, and Colossians*, trans. T. H. L. Parker, ed. David W. Torrance and Thomas F. Torrance (Grand Rapids, MI: Wm. B. Eerdmans Publishing Co., 1965), 142.

4. Joyce Rupp, *Prayer* (Maryknoll, NY: Orbis Books, 2007), 62.

5. Adrian van Kaam, *Spirituality and the Gentle Life* (Pittsburgh, PA: Epiphany Association, 1994), 52.

6. William Johnston, *The Mysticism of the Cloud of Unknowing* (Saint Meinrad, IN: Abbey Press, 1975), 174.

7. Calvin, *Institutes*, 854.

8. Andrew Murray, *The Deeper Christian Life: A Modern Interpretation*, 2nd ed. (Grand Rapids, MI: Fleming H. Revell, 1895), http://www.ccel.org/ccel/murray/deeper.txt

9. Thomas Keating, *The Method of Centering Prayer, The Prayer of Consent* brochure (Butler, NJ: Contemplative Outreach, 2006), www.contemplativeoutreach.org.

10. George Macdonald, *Diary of an Old Soul: 366 Writings for Devotional Reflection* (Minneapolis, MN: Augsburg Publishing House, 1975), 114.

DAY 1 BREATH OF GOD

1. From William J. Petersen and Randy Petersen, *The One Year Book of Hymns*, comp. and ed. Robert K. Brown and Mark R. Norton (Wheaton, IL: Tyndale House Publishers, 1995), August 28.

DAY 5 NOTICING

1. Nan C. Merrill, *Friends of Silence* XXII, no. 7 (July/August 2009):1.

DAY 7 CALLING

1. Frederick Buechner, *Wishful Thinking: A Seeker's ABC*, rev. ed. (San Francisco: HarperSanFrancisco, 1993), 119.

DAY 10 INSPIRATION

1. John of the Cross, *Dark Night of the Soul*, 3rd ed., trans. and ed. E. Allison Peers (Garden City, NY: Image Books, 1959), 100.

2. See Raymond E. Brown, *The Gospel According to John* (New York: Doubleday, 1970), 1022–23. "Lootfy Levonian, *The Expositor*, 8th Series, 22 (1921), 149–54, discussing such beliefs and practices in relation to John xx 22, says (with confidence!) of the latter custom: 'No one can doubt apostolic succession when it comes in this form.' "

DAY 11 EXHALATION

1. Teresa of Ávila, *The Interior Castle*, trans. Kieran Kavanaugh and Otilio Rodriguez (New York: Paulist Press, 1979), 86.

2. Gayle Boss, *Weavings: A Journal of the Christian Spiritual Life*, 23, no. 1 (January/February 2008):18.

DAY 12 LETTING GO

1. Quoted in C. S. Lewis, *The Problem of Pain* (New York: Macmillan, 1944), 84.

2. Charles Honey, "Grand Rapids Artist Finds Sacred Connection," *The Grand Rapids Press* (Saturday, July 12, 2008), section C, 1–2.

3. John P. Varineau, *The Grand Rapids Symphony* playbill vol. I (2008–2009 season), 57.

DAY 13 CONFESSION

1. *The Service for the Lord's Day: The Worship of God: Supplemental Liturgical Resource 1* (Philadelphia, PA: Westminster Press, 1984), 48.

DAY 15 BANISHING FEAR

1. Nan C. Merrill, *Psalms for Praying: An Invitation to Wholeness* (New York: Continuum Publishing, 1999), 119.

DAY 16 DISPELLING ANXIETY

1. Howard Thurman, *Meditations of the Heart* (New York: Harper & Row Publishers, 1953), 28–29.

2. John Baillie, *A Diary of Private Prayer* (New York: Charles Scribner's Sons, 1949), 55.

DAY 17 LETTING GO OF ESTEEM

1. John Calvin, *Golden Booklet of the True Christian Life*, trans. Henry J. Van Andel (Grand Rapids, MI: Baker Books, 1952), 20, 21, 22.

DAY 18 DETACHMENT

1. *The Philokalia*, comp. St. Nikodimos of the Holy Mountain and St. Makarios of Corinth, trans. G. E. H. Palmer, Philip Sherrard, and Kallistos Ware (London: Faber and Faber, 1979), 1:55–71.

2. *Writings from the Philokalia on Prayer of the Heart*, trans. E. Kadloubovsky and G. E. H. Palmer (London: Faber and Faber, 1951), 92, 155–61.

DAY 19 EMPTIED

1. Cynthia Bourgeault, *Centering Prayer and Inner Awakening* (Cambridge, MA: Cowley Publications, 2004), 88.

2. Thomas Keating, *Open Mind, Open Heart* (New York: Continuum, 2006), 66.

3. Steven Chase, *The Tree of Life: Models of Christian Prayer* (Grand Rapids, MI: Baker Academic, 2005), 176.

DAY 20 SELFLESS

1. John of the Cross, *Living Flame of Love*, trans. and ed. E. Allison Peers (New York: Triumph Books, 1991), 71, 77.

2. Ibid., 78.

3. Murray, *Deeper Christian Life*, http://www.ccel.org/ccel/murray/deeper.

4. Bernadette Roberts, *The Path to No-Self: Life at the Center* (Albany, NY: State University of New York Press, 1991), 197.

5. Ibid., 200–205.

DAY 21 GLORIFICATION

1. Often attributed to Nelson Mandela, this was written by Marianne Williamson in *A Return to Love: Reflections on the Principles of A Course in Miracles* (New York: Harper Perennial, 1992), 191.

DAY 22 LITTLE CHRISTS

1. Martin Luther, *Works of Martin Luther*, vol. 2 (Philadelphia, PA: Muhlenberg Press, 1943), 338.

2. C. S. Lewis, *Mere Christianity* (New York: Collier Books/Macmillan Publishing Company, 1960), 155.

3. Ibid., 49.

4. Ibid., 174–175

5. Allen O. Miller and M. Eugene Osterhaven, trans., *The Heidelberg Catechism*, 400th Anniversary Edition (New York: United Church Press, 1962), 9.

DAY 23 PRAYING THROUGH THE PAIN

1. John of the Cross, *Dark Night of the Soul*, 61.

2. Ibid., 63–69.

3. Ibid., 103–108.

4. Ibid., 70–71.

DAY 25 CONTEMPLATION

1. *The Cloud of Unknowing*, ed. James Walsh (New York: Paulist Press, 1981), 120–21.

2. Steven Chase, *Contemplation and Compassion: The Victorine Tradition* (Maryknoll, NY: Orbis Books, 2003), 149.

3. Thomas R. Kelly, *A Testament of Devotion* (San Francisco: HarperSanFrancisco, 1992), 38, 73.

DAY 26 TRUSTING GOD

1. Jean-Pierre de Caussade, *The Sacrament of the Present Moment*, trans. Kitty Muggeridge (San Francisco, HarperSanFrancisco, 1989), 10–11.

2. *The Welcoming Prayer* brochure (Butler, NJ: Contemplative Outreach, www.contemplativeoutreach.org).

DAY 27 THE AROMA OF CHRIST

1. http://en.wikipedia.org/wiki/Perfume access date 7/22/09.

2. Origen, "On the Incarnation of Christ" in http://library.Thinkquest.org/3750/smell.html

3. Philip Schaff, *Ante-Nicene Fathers: Tertullian, Part Fourth; Minucius Felix;*

Commodian; Origen, Parts First and Second (Grand Rapids, MI: Wm. B. Eerdmans Publishing, n.d.) 4:284. http://www.ccel.org/ccel/schaff/anf04.i.html

4. Augustine, *Confessions of Saint Augustine*, trans. Edward B. Pusey (Oak Harbor, WA: Logos Research Systems, 1999), bk. 10, chap. 27. http://www.ccel.org/ccel/augustine/confess.xi.xxvii.html

5. *John Henry Newman, Heart Speaks to Heart*, ed. Lawrence Cunningham (Hyde Park, NY: New City Press, 2004), 47–48.

DAY 28 WIND

1. Thomas H. Troeger, "Wind Who Makes All Winds that Blow," stanza 1.

DAY 29 FIRE

1. Albert N. Wells, *Pascal's Recovery of Man's Wholeness* (Richmond, VA: John Knox Press, 1965), 92.

2. John of the Cross, *Living Flame of Love*, Prologue (New York: Triumph Books, 1991), 17.

3. John of the Cross, *Dark Night of the Soul*, 72.

4. Thomas H. Troeger, "Wind Who Makes All Winds that Blow," stanzas 2–3.

DAY 33 COMMUNITY

1. Thurman, *Meditations of the Heart*, 121.

2. Timothy Koock, quoted in Mary Anne Best, *Community: Oneness in Contemplation* (Butler, NJ: Contemplative Outreach, 2008), 30.

3. Thomas R. Ward Jr., "Spirituality and Community: Centering Prayer and the Ecclesial Dimension," in Thomas Keating and others, *The Divine Indwelling: Centering Prayer and Its Development* (New York: Lantern Books, 2001), 17.

4. Best, *Community*, 15.

5. Thomas Keating, *Manifesting God* (New York: Lantern Books, 2005), 108.

6. Dorothy Day, "Room for Christ," *The Catholic Worker* 12, no. 10 (December 1945):2.

DAY 34 CHURCH

1. Calvin, *Institutes of the Christian Religion*, ed. John T. McNeill, trans. Ford Lewis Battles, vol. 21 (Philadelphia, PA: Westminster Press, 1960), 1369.

2. Ibid., 1370.

DAY 35 PRAYING CONSTANTLY

1. For assistance in forming an "active prayer" see pages 171–72 in *Open Mind, Open Heart* by Thomas Keating and read suggestions for a "breath prayer" in *The Breath of Life* by Ron DelBene.

DAY 36 GRATITUDE

1. Karl Barth, *Church Dogmatics*, vol. 4, *The Doctrine of Reconciliation,* ed. G. W. Bromiley and T. F. Torrance (Edinburgh: T. & T. Clark, 1956), 41.

2. *The Heidelberg Catechism*, 11.

3. Ibid., 87.

DAY 37 ONE WITH I AM

1. Teresa of Ávila, *Interior Castle*, trans. E. Allison Peers (Garden City, NY: Image Books, 1961), 38.

2. *The Heidelberg Catechism*, 9.

3. Thomas Keating, quoted in Best, *Community*, 112–13.

DAY 38 CRUCIFIED

1. John Wesley, *A Plain Account of Christian Perfection*, vol. 11, The Works of John Wesley, ed. by Thomas Jackson (n.p.: 1872), http://www.ccel. org/ccel/wesley/perfection/files/perfection.html

BIBLIOGRAPHY

Caussade, Jean-Pierre de. *A Treatise on Prayer from the Heart: A Christian Mystical Tradition Recovered for All.* Translated, edited, and introduced by Robert M. McKeon. Saint Louis, MO: Institute of Jesuit Sources, 1998.

Chase, Steven. *The Tree of Life: Models of Christian Prayer.* Grand Rapids, MI: Baker Academic, 2005.

DelBene, Ron, Herb Montgomery, and Mary Montgomery. *The Breath of Life: A Simple Way to Pray.* Eugene, OR: Wipf and Stock Publishers, 2005.

Hall, Thelma. *Too Deep for Words: Rediscovering Lectio Divina.* Mahwah, NJ: Paulist Press, 1988.

Keating, Thomas. *Open Mind, Open Heart: The Contemplative Dimension of the Gospel.* New York: Continuum, 2006.

Keating, Thomas, and others. *Spirituality, Contemplation & Transformation: Writings on Centering Prayer.* 20th anniversary edition. New York: Lantern Books, 2008.

————, et al. *The Divine Indwelling: Centering Prayer and Its Development.* New York: Lantern Books, 2001.

Kelly, Thomas R. *A Testament of Devotion.* San Francisco: HarperSanFrancisco, 1992.

Kinn, James W. *The Practice of Contemplation According to John of the Cross.* Washington, DC: ICS Publications, 2009.

Merton, Thomas. *New Seeds of Contemplation.* New York: New Directions Books, 1961.

Muyskens, J. David. *Forty Days to a Closer Walk with God: The Practice of Centering Prayer.* Nashville, TN: Upper Room Books, 2006.

Pennington, M. Basil. *Centered Living: The Way of Centering Prayer.* Liguori, MO: Liguori/Triumph, 1999.

Roberts, Bernadette. *The Path to No-Self: Life at the Center.* Albany, NY: State University of New York Press, 1991.

ABOUT THE AUTHOR

J. DAVID MUYSKENS, a retired minister of the Reformed Church in America and a seminary teacher, is a graduate of Northwestern and Central Colleges in Iowa, Western Theological Seminary in Michigan, and has Th.M. and D.Min. degrees from Princeton Theological Seminary. He served as pastor of three churches in New Jersey and adjunct professor of spirituality at New Brunswick Theological in New Jersey. He has been a spiritual director since 1991 and is a graduate of the Spiritual Guidance Program of the Shalem Institute in Bethesda, Maryland.

He has been practicing Centering Prayer since 1993 and has facilitated a Centering Prayer group since 2001. In 1999 Reverend Muyskens was commissioned by Contemplative Outreach as a presenter of Centering Prayer. From 2002 to 2008 he was coordinator of the West Michigan chapter of the West Michigan chapter of Contemplative Outreach. Currently he is a member of the Circle of Service of Contemplative Outreach as the coordinator of the International Service Team.

Reverend Muyskens has authored several books and numerous articles. He is married, has a son, two daughters, and five grandchildren. His interests include genealogy and wood carving.